TRUE TO THE EARTH

PAGAN POLITICAL THEOLOGY

KADMUS

True to the Earth:
Pagan Political Theology

ISBN
978-1-7325523-1-9

First Printed
by Gods&Radicals Press 2018

Cover Design by Li Pallas
Li.pallas.loves.you.com

Layout by Casandra Johns
Houseofhands.com

Editing Team
Rhyd Wildermuth
Casandra Johns

Gods&Radicals Press
PO Box 11850
Olympia, Washington 98508

Solidarity, bulk discount, and wholesale copies available

Contact the editors or author at
Editor@Godsandradicals.org

Or for distro contact us at
Distro@ABeautifulResistance.com

Gods&Radicals Press is a not-for-profit anti-capitalist Pagan publisher.
View our works and online journal at:
Abeautifulresistance.org

ACKNOWLEDGMENTS

Many people made this book possible but I would like to give special thanks to Dr. Al Cummins, Mallorie Vaudoise, Peter Leykam, and Jesse Hathaway for numerous rich and helpful conversations and other opportunities to learn from them. Rhyd Wildermuth has provided extraordinary help and unflagging support. Finally, I would like to thank my husband and all my friends who encourage and inspire my work.

"I beseech you, my brothers, remain faithful to the earth and do not believe those who speak to you of extraterrestrial hopes! They are mixers of poisons whether they know it or not...

Now to desecrate the earth is the most terrible thing, and to esteem the bowels of the unfathomable higher than the meaning of the earth!"

Nietzsche, *Thus Spoke Zarathustra*

CONTENTS

INTRODUCTION
Why This Book?

We can little conceive how different life now appears to us than it did to our ancestors. While much of value has been gained, some of humanity's most vital and precious treasures have been lost. What we could call a pagan worldview or a polytheist perspective once allowed us to see and think things which have now become invisible to us, or available only with great and circuitous effort. The pages that follow are an attempt to reclaim and return to this lost perspective. It is a perspective now so distant from our experiences that we fail to even feel the wound of what has gone.

There are great obstacles here. Our modern culture, philosophy, science, politics, and of course common religion are so thoroughly integrated with a monotheistic foundation that we often cannot recognize this integration and its source. But there is another obstacle even greater than this: our literate societies.

Pagan cultures were originally oral societies without writing, and contemporary pagan cultures were largely oral until the introduction of writing via violent colonialism and monotheist missionary campaigns. The surviving written documents from ancient pagan cultures are also frequently the last documents of cultures crushed through monotheist invasion. When this isn't the case, as in Ancient Greece, the development of writing brings its own challenges, particularly conceptual and cognitive changes which obscure the previous insights that formed the heart of pagan culture.

Whether we are dealing with documentary evidence of a pagan culture (whether first-hand documentation of a surviving culture or written records from a lost culture capturing a fading way of life,) we inevitably find layers of alteration which distort our understanding. These alterations can be inadvertent, often caused by the blind spots of the writer, and overt, including alterations due to the prejudices and colonial project of the scribe. Whether caused by scribes who added Christianity to *Beowulf* or the anthropologists who felt the need to interpret the teachings of the people they studied in terms of "what they would have said if they had the language," what we inherit has been distorted in the direction of a literate and/or a monotheistic worldview, worldviews which differ dramatically from pagan culture at its prime.

Despite these difficulties, we have very urgent reasons to do the work of recovering these radically different worldviews. We live in a time of multiple growing and interconnected crises, each with political deadlocks which prevent us from addressing these crises effectively or in any meaningful way at all. The most obvious of these is the climate crisis. It is a crisis which threatens the entire world, one which has already caused extensive destabilization and loss of life and joy, and one which disproportionately affects the poorest and least powerful of the world's nations and inhabitants first and worst, despite their very minimal role in causing this crisis.

We consider this disaster, overtly or otherwise, most commonly in terms of cost-value analysis. How many lives can be lost, how many islands drowned or communities starved, before the bottom line of international corporate interests should be inconvenienced? Every human life, every dying forest and blighted sea, has a price. Ultimately, the very real danger appears unreal to us; we are too often assuaged by the power and control, the very cause of this crisis, which our modern scientific and economic approaches has granted us. The world, our current view assumes, is a coal mine, a gas station, and it simply requires better management and perhaps a few new technological breakthroughs to save it.

The crisis of climate change cannot be divided from the cancerous nature of a society based on the need of unending growth. Profits, production, consumption, technological power, all of this must grow lest the fundamental structures of our society collapse. What this imperative overlooks is obvious: the only things that grow indefinitely destroy their environments and eventually themselves.

We also face financial inequalities that are in many nations the worst they have been within a century. These are far worse than they initially appear: an impossibly ballooning debt system has obscured inequality for two generations. This is not a surface or accidental phenomenon. The growth in technology has gone hand in hand with the elimination of previous jobs, and no society which insists on employment as the only means to survive can sustain any level of economic fairness in the face of technological advance.

A society can, however, postpone the inevitable collapse through an increase in unnecessary bureaucratic jobs and an ever-ballooning system of debt. Debt allows utterly unaffordable houses, cars, computers, cell-phones, and even life necessities to continue to sell. Debt allows astronomically expensive schools to remain in existence. Debt allows everyday people to convince themselves they are living well when really they are all collectively living on borrowed time.[1] As with the earth's resources, we have borrowed today from a future that does not exist. After more than fifty years of debt compensating for rising prices, now even minimum payments can no longer be made. This is an essential crisis of the world economy that has been put off, time and again, by short-term illusory solutions.

Consumption and acquisition have a compulsory, compulsive, and pathological character in our contemporary world. Having lost meaning we are reduced to amassing. By psychological and sociological metrics, we are miserable. We cling to the only thing we have; the siren call of *more*. But the crises are real, though they take different forms in different cultures and countries. Countries with strong histories of providing for the social welfare of their peoples find their safety nets cut through harsh austerity policies at the behest of international financial concerns. Countries lacking these systems of social support find the already precarious lives of their people made even more uncertain and endangered.

As our tentative perch on the edge of the cliff crumbles around us, people focus their attention instead—either through the machinations of those with the most to lose or through their own misguided impulses—to deeply imbedded social tensions. Rather than looking to systems whose foundations have always been exploitative and unsustainable, racist and xenophobic fantasies dominate the vision. More and more people believe that immigrants and minorities are taking advantage of a system that was never even designed to provide a reasonable life to all—or even most—of those who lived within it.

---

1   As David Graeber points out in *Debt: The First 5000 Years*, the world's debt exceeds several times over the entire wealth of the earth. These debts cannot be paid, and if they could be such repayment would cause an economic collapse for the massive segment of our economies which depend on interest for these debts for their incomes. This requires a continued system of debt-slavery in which people continue making minimum payments on debts they will never discharge to enjoy "property" they will never really own.

Fascism rises, offering order and control, a return to a past that was always an illusion and a lie for most people.

It turns out democracy and rights were always optional, but the proper running of the machine, the reduction of people and the earth to their market price and place, never was. If we do not address the inadequacies in our understanding of the cosmos, the blind spots which keep us from seeing the historical challenges that face us, then fascism, as it has so often before, will simplify the efficiency of the system in its own bloody final manner.

In the face of such deadly peril, we need to expand our vision of what life could be.

Pagan Metaphysics

The questions of this project are two-fold. First, what constitutes a pagan metaphysics? Second, what can a pagan metaphysics contribute to our understanding of reality and attempts to address the challenges we currently face? The first question will focus on a reclamation of a pagan metaphysics, the second on what this metaphysics has to tell us about ethics and politics. This second matter should make clear that our goal is not to understand something ancient and original simply because it is so. I engage in this endeavor with one eye to the deep value a truly pagan worldview can make available to us, and with one eye to potential dangers, shortcomings, and blind spots. This is not an uncritical project, but rather an evaluative one.

I have thus far already been using several different names and terms that require clarification. I am seeking to uncover a metaphysics that can be found, to a greater or less extent (and with important variations) throughout what I have been calling pagan cultures. I have not made much use of the word "religion" and do not really intend to. Religion is an infamously difficult concept to define, and it is a concept that pagan cultures generally did not have.

Historically, the term "religion" is embroiled very early on in a war between monotheism and polytheism, and the most common understanding of the term derives from a monotheistic re-invention of older pagan Latin concepts. The Roman philosopher and statesman Cicero was one of the first to formulate a clear use of the term "religion," tracing the word "religion" to the verb *relegere*, which meant "to re-read or re-trace." Religion in this understanding is a return to and respect for the ancestors and traditional teachings.

In Rome, these teachings and traditions were, of course, pagan. With the rise of Christianity in Rome, however, religion was redefined to allow it to reject adherence to the pagan ancestral traditions. The third century AD Christian writer Lactantius rejected Cicero's understanding and claimed instead that "religion" comes from *re-ligare*, "to bind together and link." This is the standard etymology most people suggest in the contemporary world, forgetting the older pagan sense of the term. For Lactantius this means that true religion is that which worships the one *truth* that binds all other truths together. Therefore, in that meaning, those who worship many gods do not engage in true religion because they reject the one binding truth and god that unifies all. So, with the word redefined, pagan or polytheistic religion became a contradiction in terms.[2]

For our purposes religion is best understood as just a part of culture, and it is more useful to focus on culture in general rather than attempting to discern within a culture what is or is not religious. Relatively few cultures have a highly-developed presentation of their own metaphysics as such; instead, we will need to discern and distill pagan metaphysics from pagan culture.

A metaphysics consists of answers to the most fundamental questions we can ask. What exists? In what way does it exist? Where did it come from? What is the nature of the cosmos? Where do we fit into what exists? What are the most important things in life and in existence? These questions are rarely overtly asked in any culture and seldom overtly answered. Instead, the asking and answering is found spread throughout all the aspects of a culture; likewise, the asking and answering are never consistent throughout an entire culture, especially when we take historical change into account. Despite that, we can find major and minor themes and enduring threads shared throughout similar types of cultures and contexts.

Even as most cultures do not have overtly developed metaphysics, even though they all have robust metaphysical understandings embedded in their way of life, most cultures do not have overt theologies. A theology is simply the clarification and development of the metaphysics housed within a culture's practices. Theology makes overt what was previously implicit. Only with the introduction of a concept of religion (understood as a specific area of practice dealing with gods or god) did theology and metaphysics become separated into apparently different, though overlapping, disciplines.

---

2   See Cicero's *De Natura Deorum* II.72, Lactantius *Institutiones Divinae* IV.28, and the discussions of this history found in both Richard King's *Orientalism and Religion: Postcolonial Theory, India and 'the Mystic East'* and Page DuBois' excellent *A Million and One Gods: The Persistence of Polytheism.*

Putting religion aside, then, we are left with the practice of theology and metaphysics as essentially the same.

Metaphysical-theological understandings provide the unavoidable and necessary basis for any and all ethics and politics. One must know what exists, how it exists, and what matters in order to answer questions about how we should behave and interact individually and collectively. It is impossible to adopt a politics or ethics without also accepting, whether knowingly or not, a metaphysics. This is as true for Liberal Democracy or Capitalism or Communism as for medieval Feudalism or ancient systems of aristocracy. One cannot adhere to a certain way of living with one another without also accepting implied answers to what our existence, and the existence of the cosmos, is like in its most fundamental aspects.

Pagan Political Theology?

Some argue that paganism has nothing to do with politics or that it should remain neutral on political questions. There are several different motivations for this position and several ways to respond to it.

On the simplest level, the statement that "paganism has nothing to do with politics" can be quickly shown as shockingly naïve and false. Understanding the earth as a living goddess has immediate implications for how we view laws concerning the ownership, use, or abuse of the earth. To think otherwise is to suggest that an analogous situation, for example understanding that a glass contains a deadly poison, has absolutely no implications for whether someone who wishes to be healthy will drink it. To have a view about what various things like humanity or the earth are, and what matters in life, is to already have a politics, even if only implicitly.

Moving to a higher level of subtlety, the position that "paganism has nothing to do with politics" sometimes involves an official adoption of a Liberal Democratic division of politics from questions about the ultimate meaning and purpose of life. In other words, one might adopt the idea that politics should not tell us what is ultimately important. If this is the case, however, the reverse also holds true: what we believe is good in politics should have nothing to do with what we believe is good in general or on a higher level. This would be just as mistaken as the previous position.

The Liberal tradition of political philosophy was only able to argue that the government should remain neutral on questions of the ultimate goods in life precisely because it was informed by a robust and highly developed metaphysics. The Liberal tradition is founded upon a decision on what the highest goods are, and one of these goods is that rational autonomy is best served through government neutrality on metaphysical questions. To adopt a stance that your own metaphysics tells you nothing about how we should live is to make a mistake that political philosophy never made.

It is, of course, true that "Apollo said so" is just as terrible an argument for a political position as "The Bible says so" Any metaphysics and theology worth taking seriously, however, will have more going for it than revelation alone. To have decided to listen to Apollo, or the Bible, and so on is already to have assessed the source of revelation in light of what we believe reality is like. Someone who really believes there is no rational ground for believing in the divine, for example, would treat their own experience of a religious revelation as a mental disorder or something similar (alien intervention, perhaps) and be done with it. The voice of a god has no power until we determine first that gods might exist and might have voices. The same point can go for the full content provided by a divine voice, or book, or prophet, and so on. Each must undergo personal critical assessment, and has indeed already been assessed (whether adequately or not) before we adopt it. This means that there is always a more robust answer available than revelation or divine dictate, and this answer is open to discussion, debate, comparison, and individual assessment.

I should note that I am not here making ethical claims or laying down rules. I am simply stating how we in fact already think. To believe something, for example that what a god says matters, is to have reasons to believe it and thus to have engaged in reasoning about it. This reasoning might be better or worse, more or less developed or explicit, and so on—but it is always present in every case.

Finally, one might reject paganism informing politics out of a concern over power. In other words, this objection embodies the desire not to have spiritual leaders telling us what to do or think politically. This is a perfectly legitimate concern, one to which I am sympathetic. The direction of this argument, however, is mistaken. If you have decided that a given person has particularly valuable insights about the nature of life and the cosmos, those insights will have political implications regardless of whether you notice or like these implications. A theological and metaphysical teaching can't help but suggest certain things about how you should live, otherwise it wouldn't actually be telling you anything at all.

The greater question here is the role of spiritual leaders and authorities in general. If one has concerns in this regard, they are better approached through engaging in continual critical engagement and assessment of the teachings considered and of the teachers encountered. If you want your politics free from the voice of external authority, keep your metaphysics and theology similarly free of external authority and you are safe. But the moment you accept any statement about the nature of the cosmos you have already accepted, no matter how minimally, various ethical and political implications.

In light of what has been said so far, I will state what should already be clear: I do not rely upon any special authority here. What I have said, and will say, I offer in terms of argumentation and interpretation of often difficult subject matters. It is for the reader to decide whether my arguments are persuasive and my interpretations valuable. In an endeavor such as this there is no room for personal authority or demands for respect beyond that owed a fellow enquirer. When addressing the question of the ultimate nature of reality and human life, the reliance upon degrees, titles, lineages, heritages, secret teachings, special initiations, or personal relationships with gods and spirits does injustice to both the subject matter and the seeker.

High Paganism, Late Paganism, and Monotheism

Some distinctions between different historical periods, more generally as phases through which many cultures have gone, are important for this project. These distinctions will always be open to more fine-grained divisions, a point which will complicate our consideration of transitional figures straddling these various periods (such as Plato), but it is important to have them in mind. These three periods or phases will be high paganism, late paganism, and monotheism.

Periods of **high paganism** are almost always entirely polytheist and entirely oral. This includes pre-writing Norse and Celtic culture, for example. It also applies to Pre-Classical Greece of the Archaic, Mycenaean, and Minoan periods. I will argue that it applies as well to most pre-colonization Native American and African cultures.

Late paganism has two transitional variations in the history of pagan culture. In Greece, we have high pagan metaphysics changed largely through the development of writing and the conceptual and cognitive alterations writing causes. On the other hand, in Europe, America, and Africa we have high pagan cultures forcefully changed through assaults from foreign powers, which also enforce new ways of thinking along with the imposition of writing. In both variations, late paganism is a period of change and transition in which high pagan ideas become re-formulated along increasingly monotheistic lines. Thus, the metaphysics of late paganism is often more in line with monotheist metaphysics than the previous properly pagan metaphysics of high paganism. This is the period that in Greece is largely instituted by Plato and Aristotle. It is the period of Neoplatonism and much of Roman history. I will clarify the complex argument as we proceed, but for now suffice it to say that late paganism contains the beginnings of monotheism, even when those cultures are officially pagan and polytheist.[3]

Finally, we find the periods of **monotheism**, dominated primarily by Christianity, Judaism, and Islam. This is not only a period of monotheist *religion*, however, but a dominance of every area of human thought by monotheist *metaphysics*. We are still in such a period: science and atheism alike owe their current formulations to a monotheist foundation.[4] Similarly, because much of our contemporary paganism resembles more the metaphysics of late paganism rather than that of high paganism, they are largely religions with polytheist or pagan aesthetics built upon monotheist foundations.

Much of this book will focus upon what we know of the high pagan culture of oral Archaic Greece and the transitions that occurred during the late pagan Classical, Hellenistic, and Roman periods. There are several reasons why Greece will shoulder so much of the burden of this texts. First I must stress that it is not because of a particular preference for this form of paganism in my own life and practice; I have deeper and much more intimate relationships with the deities of the Celts. However, Greece is the stage in which we have the most extensive and careful record of the transition from oral to literate society, as well as the transition from high paganism to late paganism. Beyond this, Greece is also the location of one of the most fully developed and intricately worked-out presentations of monotheistic metaphysics and its arguments against a pagan metaphysics. The later dominance of monotheistic metaphysics elsewhere in the world comes largely from the success of the work of Plato and Aristotle. For these reasons, Greece necessarily plays a central role in our investigation.

---

3   Here it is also important to note that most contemporary pagan and neo-pagan thought owes its
    origins to late paganism; it therefore tends to be based on a monotheistic or proto-monotheistic
    metaphysics, such as that of Plato.

4   This is not to say they are cannot be reformulated atop different foundations.

What Is Meant by Pagan?

As a final note on terminology, you will have noticed that I fluctuate between using the terms "pagan" and "polytheist." In recent years movements like Devotional Polytheism have worked to make more precise and technical the distinction between paganism and polytheism in order to distinguish between two types of views on the gods: those who believe in the literal reality and independent existence of gods, versus those who adopt a variety of views in which they are not independent and actually-existing (for instance: archetypes, faces of a singular entity, or symbols of cosmic forces, etc.). Previously, "polytheist" was a technical term within academia for the belief in many gods while "pagan" was derided due to its history as originating as a slur.

I am sensitive to both the goals of those who wish to insist on the independent reality of the gods and those who are concerned with the hateful history of the term pagan. However, as the title of this work attests, I prefer the term "pagan" to "polytheist," but my use of "pagan" is not meant to reject the concerns of those who self-identify as polytheist. I prefer this usage for three reasons. First, polytheism has far too technical a sound and feel to replace the poetic force of the word "pagan." Second, "pagan" derives from the Latin term for "rustic" or "connected to the countryside." While it was used to mean something like the slur "hick," it does end up capturing the closeness of pagan culture to the earth and nature. This aspect of the meaning of "pagan" is worth embracing.[5] Finally, not all the cultures I will refer to as pagan will perfectly fit the label polytheist, and the less technically restricted term "pagan" will allow me more freedom to capture what I feel are the most powerful aspects of high pagan culture.

This project draws out key points from cultures that have been found throughout the globe and throughout history, though many of them hail from iron and bronze age historical periods. Some of these points will be central to most of the cultures under discussion, and some of them could be, I argue, particularly important for us. There is always a danger, and not a negligible one, in generalizing over many cultures and historical time periods.

---

5   It is also worth noting that while the term *polytheos* does indeed show up in Ancient Greek to mean "belonging to many gods" for example in Aeschylus' play, *The Suppliant Women,* it was likely first used in English in the seventeenth century as a term used by Protestants to attack Catholics. Thus, the Protestant Samuel Purchas described what was offered by Catholic missionaries to the peoples of Asia as "an exchanged Polytheisme in worshipping of Saints, Images, and the Host." Samuel Purchas as quoted in Page DuBois, *A Million and One Gods: The Persistence of Polytheism* (Cambridge, MA: Harvard University Press, 2014), 20. In other words, "polytheism" has been primarily used as just as much a slur as "pagan."

This risks reducing or dismissing the rich and complex differences between cultures, as is often done when religion and mythology is interpreted in light of general archetypes. This is absolutely not my intention and I take it as a given that the rich differences between cultures are often more important than their similarities. This will go as well for the forms of monotheism across which I will also be generalizing. This is why it will be important that I will be discussing the metaphysics found within or behind a religion, rather than the details and specifics of religions in particular.

I will be approaching the subject with a different methodology from that frequently used by Jung and others in arguing for the existence of archetypes. The path that frequently leads to generalizations about archetypes across cultures is the recognition (or the assumption) of commonality in myths or gods, followed by the proposal of a psychological or metaphysical basis for these commonalities. These commonalities are not justified beyond the level of observations and descriptions which are themselves highly sensitive to starting assumptions and biases. This book, however, is ultimately inspired by shared cultural and psychological mechanisms that leads us to expect conceptual commonalities. Specifically, the fact that all pagan cultures originate in oral cultures allows us to hypothesize that orality provides the foundation for key conceptual commonalities.

How This Book Is Organized

I will conclude this introduction with a note about the organization of this book. The main argument occurs in the labeled chapters. In between these chapters are interludes where I explore literary and mythological themes that provide interesting and useful examples of the larger points I am making. While these interludes add context and color to the argument, you can follow the main argument by reading the chapters alone if you wish. Alternatively, the interludes can stand as independent essays on their own.

CHAPTER ONE
Preliminaries to a Pagan Metaphysics

Ametaphysics is like a lens through which we see the world. It is the water of the sea of meaning in which we swim, informing our every choice, feeling, and experience.

When something happens that makes me angry, I get angry because the event is experienced as something that "should not be." It is experienced in this way because we already have an idea, a commitment, to a certain picture of how things are and how they ought to be. We have a set of values, of things we love and things that speak to us, which are all part of our implicit metaphysics.

Like the lenses of eyeglasses we have worn all our lives, it is easy to never notice that we even have a metaphysics. Thus, we are seeking to understand a different lens than the one (knowingly or not) we already wear. This is no easy task, because our current metaphysics, a thoroughly monotheistic one, is already in the way.

We must approach high pagan metaphysics from two directions. We must think our way towards it through texts, legends, and historical knowledge of the times and places where it existed. This includes an investigation of oral societies and their common modes of thought. We must also think our way back from how things already appear to us within our monotheistic framework to how things would be with aspects of this framework removed.

These two approaches rely one upon the other. We must always think our way back from our context into another to understand the texts, legends, or historical information we seek to interpret. Our preliminary understanding will then open to re-evaluation based on what else we have learned through our investigation of a pagan metaphysics. This becomes a hermeneutic circle: we start with a preliminary sense of what we are seeking as a guide, and then use what we find to improve our preliminary understanding.

Cosmos, Order, and Chaos

Let us start with a word I have already used several times, "cosmos."

This word may seem slightly odd, even old-fashioned; the term "universe" is much more common in our contemporary world. The term "cosmos" is of Ancient Greek origin and shows up as far back as Homer, thus attesting to its use during the high pagan Archaic and Mycenaean periods. Our more common term, "universe," is of Latin Roman origin.[6] The difference between the two introduces us to a core idea of pagan metaphysics.

"Universe" consists of two Latin elements, the familiar *uni-* representing oneness and the less familiar *verse*. *Verse* means to "turn," which shows the clear connection between the idiom "turn of phrase" and the idea of verse in songs and poetry. Each verse is a turn, a cycle, of the song or poem. Universe means, rather literally, what has been "turned into one" or "unified." The universe is one story.

The term *cosmos* is a bit less straightforward. It was used in Homer to mean primarily "order," "rank," arrangement," and finally the whole of an arranged reality: that is, the Cosmos.[7] However, the term likely derives from a fascinating conceptual transformation of older terms. To get *kosmos* as "order" we first need the verb *komeo*, meaning "to take care of or tend." When we consider the pre-history of languages we find nouns deriving from more active verbs, and not vice versa. Oral languages before the rise of writing prioritize concrete action and only arrive at general names for things from the individual actions with which they are associated. So, we have the idea of "tending" and only later the noun for "the tended" or "the ordered." *Komeo*, "to tend," is in the Ionian dialect and likely draws upon a still older set of words from mainland Greece. These words are *komao* and *kome*.

Kome is likely the origin of *komao*, so let's tackle that first. *Kome* refers to hair, and most specifically to the flowing manes of horses. From the flow-

---

6 Many of our central and monotheistic concepts are of Latin origin. Latin's heavy influence upon world culture began during its own late pagan period, when monotheistic metaphysics was beginning to dominate the whole of the Mediterranean.

7 Homer represents the oldest Greek thought to which we have direct access through writing.

ing manes of horses, the term then comes to refer to long styled hair in men. *Komao* means to grow your hair long, but also to be decorated, plumed, ornamented and, finally, to be showy or arrogant. The order of *kosmos* comes, then, through the path of something being arranged or styled like ornaments or a long flowing mane.

So, the sense of "order" in cosmos is not one of unity, but rather one of added decoration, embellishment, and so on. It is the order that arises from growth, not unification and reduction, with the priority placed on multiplicity. The term "universe" is the exact opposite: it represents an absolute unity and reduction to oneness.

Monotheism is reductive while paganism is productive. The first reduces all things to One ultimate basis, the other derives all things from an abundant plurality. A pagan metaphysics will see everything that exists as a *cosmos*, while a monotheist one will instead see a *universe*. Reality within pagan metaphysics is defined in terms of multiplicity and complexity, while monotheism instead posits an ultimate oneness arrived at through reduction and simplification. For most versions of monotheism, the oneness of the universe will derive from the power and oneness of its creator. If god is one, then so too are Truth and Reality. On the other hand, if the gods are many, then so too are the truths of reality.

One way to understand this aspect of pagan metaphysics is that it follows a logic of "and, also." This is captured in the formulaic response appearing at the end of most of the Homeric Hymns: "And now I will remember you and another song also." In the chain of the hymns there is always "and another song also." Since these hymns are each dedicated to a divinity, this means that there is always another goddess or god.

We see this structure very clearly in Hesiod's *Theogony*, in which the cosmos is constructed out of an endless chain of reproducing divinities. I will quote at length the beginning of the genealogy of the gods offered by Hesiod to make the point clear:

> In the beginning there was only Chaos, the Abyss,
> But then Gaia, the Earth, came into being,
> Her broad bosom the ever-firm foundation of all,
> And Tartaros, dim in the underground depths,
> And Eros, the loveliest of all the Immortals, who
> Makes their bodies (and men's bodies) go limp,
> Mastering their minds and subduing their wills.

> From the Abyss were born Erebos and Dark Night.
> And Night, pregnant after sweet intercourse
> With Erebos, gave birth to Aether and Day.
>
> Earth's first child was Ouranos, starry Heaven,
> Just her size, a perfect fit on all sides.
> And a firm foundation for the blessed gods.
> And she bore the Mountains in long ranges, haunted
> By the Nymphs who live in the deep mountain dells.
> Then she gave birth to the barren, raging Sea
> Without any sexual love. But later she slept with
> Ouranos and bore Ocean with its deep currents,
> And also: Koios, Krios, Hyperion, Iapetos,
> Theia, Rheia, Themis, Mnemosyne,
> Gold-crowned Phoibe and lovely Tethys.
> After them she bore a most terrible child,
> Kronos, her youngest, an arch-deceiver,
> And this boy hated his lecherous father.[8]

The first gods arise from the abyss ("Chaos," here, has the sense of "chasm" or gaping void) on their own. These are Gaia the Earth, Eros or Sexual Desire, and Tartaros the Dark Beneath the Earth. From here, existence explodes into an ever-branching forest of new births. Some of these births occur through the fecundity of one parent alone, as is the case with Gaia's first child Ouranos or Heaven. Others, like the children of Earth and Heaven or the children of Night and Erebos, are born through sexual intercourse.

The story continues from here with successive generations each playing out their own dramas and struggles for power. Kronos, the youngest of the Titans or children of Gaia, will overthrow his own father Ouranos with the help of his mother because of Ouranos' continual rape of Gaia and refusal to allow her children to be born. Kronos, in turn, will couple with Rheia and give birth to a third generation of gods amongst whom the youngest, Zeus, will once again overthrow his father to become leader of the gods.

Note that the order of the cosmos is not one in which a first and ultimate origin point provides the structure for the whole. Instead, the most important gods of both high and late pagan Greece are late-comers in the story and are frequently illegitimate according to traditional standards of descent and

---

8   Hesiod and Stanley Lambardo, *Works and Days and Theogony* (Indianapolis: Hackett Publishing Company, 1993), 116–39.

authority. Neither Kronos nor Zeus are first born, and the ruling order of the Olympian gods represents a third generation of divinity. Beyond this, there are legends and traditions that Zeus himself would eventually face his own downfall, despite having delayed it for a time through stratagems we will consider later.

This is the logic of "and, also." The authority of the gods and the origin of the cosmos cannot be traced back to one ultimate power. Even the fundamental nature of sexual desire implied in the early birth of Eros is itself de-centered by the many births occurring without sexual intercourse. Eros is a powerful force within this cosmology, one of the most powerful, but it is not the ultimate answer to the question of the nature of the cosmos. A similar point can be made concerning gender. Eros is not distributed according to gender lines, even as reproduction is not limited to sexual reproduction, and gender lines themselves are fluid and increasingly complex.

The nature of this cosmos is plural and has no ultimate final principle nor source. It is an-archic, in the sense of lacking an ultimate *arche* or ruling principle and origin. In other words, the cosmos which is both made of the gods and takes its origin from them has sources but no source. It has meanings and powers, but never one meaning or power. It has truths but no Truth.

Norse mythology presents us with a similar story where the cosmos arises from fairly simple pre-existing conditions and increases in complexity as time goes on. Once more, the ruling divinities of the Norse are relative late-comers: even Odin himself is several generations removed from the earliest living divinities. Before Odin there is the great frost giant Ymir and a cosmic cow, along with several other giants born from Ymir's body. If we count Ymir as the first generation, Odin occupies the fourth.

Plurality in the Pagan Cosmos

The pagan cosmos is made up of ever growing lists and incomplete pieces. The pagan cosmos consists of *parts without wholes*.[9] The worlds of the Norse were partially constructed out of the parts of Ymir's body: existence was literally pieced together from divine, incomplete parts. The same is the case with the Babylonian goddess Tiamat, whose dismembered body constitutes heaven and earth. Similar legends existed in Greece in which the cosmos,

---

9   This is also a key aspect of thinking within an oral culture, but we will discuss this point more fully later.

or sometimes humanity, are understood to have been shaped from the body of Ouranos, Kronos, or sometimes the Titans in general. Pieces giving birth to new pieces while themselves undergoing change and being re-purposed with time: this is the logic of the many.

Consider how different this is from what we find described in *Genesis*. There, in the beginning, is the One. That One is alone with the void, and creates everything out of nothingness. The original One is also the most important entity. The whole of existence is reducible to this One, and ultimately this One is what matters. All power, truth, and meaning ultimately originate from and return to this One.

This point is even clearer when we view the nature of this One's creative power: it creates via speech and thought. From the very start we see a distancing from the body and from the complicated irreducible nature of the body. Where other gods are born and give birth, the One speaks and it is so. If we also consider the connection between speech and meaning, we see that, unlike in pagan cosmologies, meaning does not rise and shift over time but rather is intended and set from the very beginning.

Unlike the growth and change implied in the concept of sexual intercourse and birth, this aspect of words fixing meaning forever is repeated in the One's granting to Adam the power to name the animals. With this naming, the nature of each thing is set for all time. This idea of meaning is found also in the god of the *Torah*'s resistance to being named. When asked for a name by Moses it says, "I am that I am," as well as identifying itself as the god of Moses' ancestors. Where we find suggestions that this god has a name, it is a name requiring secrecy and protection.

The pagan gods, on the other hand, are not reducible to one name; rather, their names multiply. There is never a sense that the "real" name of Odin or Zeus is to be kept hidden or that those names contain great power. To *be* Odin or Zeus is to have many names, and to be open to taking on many more. Within pagan metaphysics, the more names and the more fertile and numerous the nature of the deity, the greater is that deity's power.

What is thought true of the divinities would also be true of the things to which those divinities give rise and over which they rule. Ultimately, to discuss the nature of divinity is to discuss the nature of reality. So, when we find cultures with multiple divinities irreducible to one ultimate deity and when, likewise, those divinities are themselves open to alteration and pluralism within their own nature, we will find a similar thinking about reality. Such thinking refuses to reduce the nature of existence to any one ultimate principle and refuses to reduce anything in existence to a singular nature. The pluralism of a pagan metaphysics applies to the cosmos and its constituents alike.

We see this irreducible, pluralistic understanding of the cosmos play out in Plato and his version of Socrates: it is what both are fighting against. Likewise, the foreignness of a non-pluralistic understanding of reality is what confuses the people who Plato presents talking to Socrates. In most cases, when Socrates asks about the nature of a thing, his partners in conversation will offer a list of examples and different types of the thing. For example, when asking about virtue, Meno begins listing the various virtues for men and women, children and servants, and so on. Socrates, however, is not pleased with this offering of a list:

> **Socrates**: How fortunate I am, Meno! When I ask you for one vir-
> tue, you present me with a swarm of them, which are in your keep-
> ing. Suppose that I carry on the figure of the swarm, and ask of you,
> What is the nature of the bee? and you answer that there are many
> kinds of bees, and I reply: But do bees differ as bees, because there
> are many and different kinds of them; or are they not rather to be
> distinguished by some other quality, as for example beauty, size, or
> shape? How would you answer me?[10]

What Socrates always seeks is a general, abstract definition of a thing's essence. In other words, Socrates is interested in finding a way to reduce the many to the One. Later this will be understood through the way a definition is supposed to capture the essence of a thing. Each thing is understood to be the *type of thing it is* because of its essence.

Aristotle presents this idea by stating that a good definition should contain the larger class a thing is a member of and the unique aspect that picks it out of the crowd. Aristotle calls this the "essential difference." Thus, for Aristotle, humans are "rational animals." We are members of the general category or class of "animals," and the *essential difference* of being rational sets us off from the group. From this view, any rational animal will by definition be human and anything without reason will not be human.

This fundamental monotheistic assumption about the nature of reality, that things can be reduced to shared ultimate natures, is also tied to a view of lan-

---

10   Plato, Benjamin Jowett, and Albert A. Anderson, *Platos Ion and Meno: Benjamin Jowetts Translation* (Millis, MA: Agora Publications, 1998).

guage. In such a view, all things identified by words or names can be reduced to a general abstract definition. To think of the world in terms of fixed essences open to general definitions is to tie the nature of reality to a characteristic of language: because the word "bee" can be defined a certain way, then so too the nature of real bees can be constrained and structured. This is one reason why Plato attempts, with varying success, to argue that the proper name of a thing must capture its nature, rather than being conventional.[11]

This only makes sense in a cosmos created from words and governed by a god that primarily speaks (and later will be understood to write). Though neither Socrates nor Plato are familiar with *Genesis*, they share a monotheistic metaphysics that causes the two paths of thought to run parallel before meeting powerfully in Gnosticism, Christianity, and Kabbalah.

These monotheistic assumptions about language are refutable. For instance, there are many types of definitions, including operative ones, that define a word in terms of the many different ways it can be used, and the contexts in which each use is appropriate. To define "bee" or "virtue" in this way would not require any discovery of the shared characteristics or essence of all bees or virtues. The twentieth-century philosopher Ludwig Wittgenstein hit upon an idea of meaning and definition that nicely fits what we find within high pagan oral cultures. For the late Wittgenstein, *a word's meaning is its use*, which in no way implies that it captures the stable unchanging natures of the things it discusses. Uses will be multiple and will continue to multiply over time.

When thinking about the nature of things in relation to the words we use to get at them, Wittgenstein offers the idea of "family resemblance." Family resemblance, as the name implies, can easily be found in most families but without there necessarily being any given aspect that all members share. There are many different shared characteristics in a family, and no one member need have all of them or any specific characteristic for the resemblance to hold. In this sense, membership in a family (including a family of things like bees, gods, or virtues) will be much like a rope. No single strand of fiber runs through an entire rope: the rope is made of many overlapping strands, none of which is universal, final, or ultimate. For a pagan metaphysics, both meaning and real natures are like this, braided like the long mane of a horse from which the word "cosmos" derives.

---

11 See Plato, *Cratylus*.

Many Truths, Many Meanings, Many Values

What holds for meanings and natures will hold for truths, values, and powers. A pagan cosmos is one without a greatest power, without a final totalizing truth, and without one ultimate value. As the gods are plural and impossible to unify in any final way, truths about reality are also multiple and irreducible. More than this, some of these truths will conflict with others, and still more will be incommensurable. Zeus and Kronos may never see eye to eye, and some aspects of reality will be impossible to understand through the lens of a given set of meanings and truths.

In a pagan cosmos, different things have to be understood through different meanings, with nothing to tie these realms or spheres of meaning together. To translate from one sphere of meaning to another will be to change, rather than to accurately capture, the truth as it exists in the original sphere of meaning.

To offer a rather simplified contemporary example (with apologies to neuroscientists), my talk of love for my husband cannot be reduced or replaced with talk of the change in chemical levels in my brain when I see him or think about him. While both descriptions are true, neither is complete and neither can be replaced by or reduced to the other. To ask, "is it ultimately love or dopamine?" is to ask an impossible and mistaken question. I can investigate whether it is love or lust. I can investigate whether we are dealing primarily with a change in dopamine or oxytocin. But I cannot test the one sphere of meaning and truth against the other.

"Ah," one might say, "but the chemical explanation will be useful for understanding and curing brain trauma or mental instability—success is its proof." Just so, but the love explanation will be far more useful for a marriage proposal, moving speech, or for crafting a meaningful life together. Standards of use and success are themselves distributed amongst spheres of truth and do not exist independent of them.

Spheres of meaning are ultimately spheres of value. To speak of truths, as indeed to speak of gods, is to ask questions and provide answers about what is important and valuable. The gods embodied different values, and those most connected to one god will identify what is important differently than those devoted to another.

This clearly has implications for ethical and political questions. There will be different ethical standards and systems to be developed from different values, and different ways of life and government appropriate for different values as well. However, the pagan world was one in which the followers of different gods and the occupants of different spheres of value most often lived with and amongst one another. This fact allows for a development of general, if tentative, principles from the nature of pagan metaphysics itself beyond the particulars of given spheres of truth.

A pagan metaphysics will be one committed to a complex plurality both in terms of types of things, truths, values, and ways of life in the cosmos, as well as the natures of individual things. The commitment to complex plurality is the reason that pagan mythology is also a story of conflict. For a pluralistic view of reality, conflict is fundamentally basic, whether it is the conflict of play or that of war.[12] The plurality of gods, and the traditions and practices of worship and value those gods teach, embrace the productive inter-relations amongst these often dramatically different forces and truths (whether those relations are friendly or more contentious.)

We see the nuanced and complicated nature of power and conflict amongst cosmic divine forces in the most basic myths of pagan culture. In order for Zeus to overthrow his father Kronos, he had to make allies amongst the Titans who were willing to provide him with the powerful lightning bolt. Without these allies and his political savvy, "wily Zeus" as he is so often called, would not have stood a chance. Similarly, Zeus' rule would have been impossible had he sought absolute power as both his father and grandfather did. Instead, the Olympians divide the world into thirds with true rulership distributed amongst Zeus in the sky, Poseidon in the seas, and Hades in the underworld. The Olympian regime is a compromise and a council, and one always in danger of breaking out into new conflict.

A similar point can be made concerning Odin. Odin's rule relies upon several things, including deals he has struck between two different families of gods, the Vanir and Aesir, establishing an uneasy alliance and a bargain with Mirmir that cost him an eye and bought him cosmic wisdom. The power of Zeus and Odin are both frequently connected to their role in protecting and enforcing promises and oaths, because it is upon this foundation of tentative agreement and alliance that their own power rests.

These points will be important when we turn to a discussion of the political implications of a pagan metaphysics. Power, in the pagan cosmos, is collective and not based in any One or Ultimate. Olympus may have a king, but his

---

12   A wholesale rejection of conflict can only be put forward by means of some one final totalizing view of how all people must behave and what values all people must share (i.e., monotheism).

throne rests on countless complex and changeable political maneuvers. This is very different from the throne of the monotheists' god, which rests upon nothing except that god's own unavoidable and unquestionable absolute power. Pagan cultures may frequently have practiced various forms of despotism, but their metaphysics and theology makes clear that the power of the despot comes from collective agreement and not individual force. There is no room for a "divine right of kings" in a pagan metaphysics, because even literally divine kings are not granted any inherent "right" to their thrones.

The actual political history of pagan cultures is a complicated and vexed subject that we will deal with in greater detail in time. What we should note now is that the nature of power and leadership is connected to the nature of wisdom and truth. We see this no clearer than in the communitarian view of the traditional African Akan culture.[13]

Akan communitarianism presents a nice counter model to the urban, empire-oriented majoritarian politics of a place like Athens. The Akan culture traditionally governed itself through communal councils made up of the leaders of the community. Each council was presided over by a leader whose primary job was to moderate the discussion of the council and execute its decisions. For this reason, Akan sayings capture such wisdom as: "There are no bad leaders, only bad advisors." Since the leader only acted on the decision of the council, any failure in action was a failure of the council.

This form of government, similar to many forms found in indigenous North American cultures, was democratic in the sense that the members of the council were representatives of the people and open to the judgment of the community should they fail in their representation. More importantly, however, these councils were overtly non-majoritarian. The aim of the council was to arrive at consensus. The councils did not recognize majority will, but rather sought to bring any points of contention to a place where each side of the issue was willing to agree. The process of council was not complete until this agreement was reached.

The belief was not that consensus arrived at the one ultimate truth, but rather that it was the best means of bringing conflicting truths into harmony. For the Akan, "one head does not go into council," making clear that council itself requires a multiple of irreducibly different views. Likewise, "wisdom does not

---

13 My knowledge of Akan thought and culture is largely drawn from the works of Kwasi Wiredu and Kwame Gyekye. For Wiredu see especially *Cultural Universals and Particulars: An African Perspective* (Bloomington: Indiana University Press, 1996). For Gyekye see especially *An Essay on African Philosophical Thought: The Akan Conceptual Scheme* (Philadelphia: Temple University Press, 1995).

reside in one head," meaning that only a collection of these different non-totalizing grasps of reality allow for wisdom.

Akan communitarianism represents the idea that, while there are many conflicting truths, wisdom is the ability to appreciate and see as many of these truths as possible without allowing any of them to dominate. While the ability to do this is limited within individuals, it is possible in a community of those seeking wisdom. There is no reduction or normalization of difference here, but rather an embrace of the productive play amongst difference. This is an insight at the very heart of a pagan metaphysics: only in plurality and difference is there truth.

FIRST INTERLUDE
Truth and Lies in a Pagan Sense

We know how to say many lies as if they were true, and when we want, we know how to speak the truth.[14]

The god whose oracle is at Delphi neither speaks plainly nor conceals, but gives a sign.[15]

But Phoibos Apollo boasted,
"Now rot here on the earth which feeds men,
at least you will no longer be an evil bane for living mortals,
who eat the fruit of the earth which nourishes many
and who will bring complete hecatombs here,
and neither Typhoeus nor accursed Chimera
shall ward off a painful death for you, but right here
the dark earth and blazing Hyperion will make you rot."
So he spoke, exulting, and darkness covered both her eyes.
And on that spot the holy force of Helios made her rot away;
Whence now it is called Pytho, and the people call
the Lord "Pythian" eponymously because there
on that spot the force of piercing Helios caused the monster to rot.
And then Phoibos Apollo knew in his heart
why the fair-flowing spring had deceived him.
And angered, he went to Telphousa and arrived at once
and stood very close to her and said to her,

---

14 The Muses speaking to Hesiod from Hesiod, Stephanie A. Nelson, Richard S. Caldwell, *Theogony ; And, Works and Days* (Newburyport, MA: Focus Publishing, 2009), 27–28.

15 Heraclitus and T.M. Robinson, *Fragments* (Toronto: Univ. of Toronto Press, 1987), fragment 93.

> *"Telphousa, you were not after all meant to deceive my mind*
> *by keeping this lovely place to pour forth your fair-flowing water.*
> *Here too indeed will my glory exist, not yours alone."*
> *He spoke and Lord Apollo the far-worker pushed her against a cliff*
> *with a shower of stones, and hid her waters,*
> *and he made an altar in the woody grove*
> *very near the fair-flowing spring. And there all men*
> *pray to the lord by the name "Telphousios"*
> *because he brought shame upon the waters of holy Telphousa."*[16]

The gods lie, steal, and deceive. This often enough drove early monotheistic thinkers away from their pagan roots. But does not nature lie and steal? Does not reality deceive? Socrates, like Descartes centuries later, argues that lies and deceit imply a lack of power and so cannot be united with the power of the divine. But it could just as well be the case that times of overabundance of power are precisely the time when deceit and theft become necessary. Faced with conflict, how does one avoid a disastrous clash of mighty powers if not through some element of clever deceit?

Lying is a type of change, especially when we recognize that the lie of a god can become a reality, just as a lie told to a god, if accepted, can become reality. Deceit and theft are just as often important aspects of how people relate to divinity as how divinities relate to us and to each other.

I began this section with three quotations. The third is taken from the story of the founding of the famous Oracle of Delphi in the longest "Homeric Hymn to Apollo." That story depicts Apollo setting up his shrine and oracle at Delphi by killing the ancient female serpent that lived there and dominating a spring, also depicted as female, who tried to convince him to place his temple elsewhere.

This story rests upon an ancient tradition that Apollo took Delphi from one or more older goddesses and replaced their worship with his own. This starkly contrasts with the hymn from the mouth of a Pythia, or prophetess, of Delphi at the beginning of Aeschylus' Eumenides:

---

16   Susan Chadwick Shelmerdine, "Homeric Hymn to Apollo," *The Homeric Hymns* (Brantford, Ont.: W. Ross MacDonald School Resource Services Library, 2008).

Pythia: *"First among the gods in this prayer I honor*
the first prophet, Earth; and after her Themis,
she who was the second to take her seat
in this place of prophecy, as a tradition tells; and third
in succession, with the consent of Themis, and with no violence done to
    any,
another Titaness, a child of Earth, took her seat here,
Phoebe. And she gave it as a birthday gift
To Phoebus; and he bears a name taken from hers."[17]

The Phoebus of the Pythia's speech is the same Phoibos Apollo of the Homeric hymn, yet these two stories could not be more different. The Homeric
Hymn I have quoted is likely from around the year 585 BC, while Aeschylus'
Eumenides was first performed in 458 BC. Thus, we are dealing with over a
century's difference in time, and we can be certain that the story depicted in
the Homeric Hymn was standard myth long before the hymn's composition.

This difference in time makes clear that it is Aeschylus who is innovating,
or perhaps who is having his fictional Pythia innovate, in this later version.
This becomes clearer when we note the stress placed on the idea of the oracle
being passed down from one prophet to another "with no violence done to
any." We can also be sure that Aeschylus is purposefully invoking a situation
of conflict amongst the gods through Apollo's relationship to the older goddesses that once ruled his oracle.

This conflict, however, is overcome through a mis-telling of the story,
through flattery, through a lie. The name of the play itself summons this
strategy of overcoming conflict through lying, misnaming, or rather renaming. The *Eumenides* means "The Kindly Ones," and refers to the least kindly of the figures in the play: the Gorgons known as the Furies or Erinyes,
whose job it is to torment those who kill their own blood relatives:

Black, altogether hateful in their ways;
and they snore with a blast unapproachable,
and from their eyes they drip a loathsome liquid.
And their attire is such as one should not bring
near to the statues of the gods nor into the houses of men.[18]

---

17 Aeschylus and Hugh Lloyd-Jones, *The Eumenides by Aeschylus* (Englewood Cliffs, NJ: Prentice-Hall, 1970), lines 1–8.
18 Aeschylus, *Eumenides*, lines 52–56.

Any magician or priestess can tell you that there is a political art involved in the praising of a divinity. Frequently we find that, the more pleasant the epithet of a god, *the more dangerous and savage the god is.* Flattering gods requires knowing which gods require which types of flattery and when that flattery should be used. The Pythia flatters Apollo by presenting his claim to Delphi as a legitimate birthday gift. The people of Athens flatter the Furies by naming them kindly and, in doing so, they help to make the Furies kindly.

Eumenides is the final of a trilogy that constitutes *The Oresteia.* This trilogy consists of the story of an increasing family tragedy that eventually threatens far more than just the human world. The first play tells the story of Agamemnon's return from the Trojan War and his murder at the hands of his wife, Clytemnestra. This is already a continuation of a cycle of death, because Clytemnestra's act is partially motivated by an action by Agamemnon before he left for war. The goddess Artemis, insulted either through an action of Agamemnon or by the foreknowledge of all who would die in the coming war, stills the winds and refuses to let the ships sail to Troy. Finally, Artemis, speaking through a priest, makes clear that the ships can only sail to Troy if Agamemnon sacrifices his daughter Iphigenia to Artemis. When Agamemnon returns, his wife has still not forgiven him for sacrificing her daughter: she kills him while he is enjoying a victorious homecoming bath. So, the father kills the daughter and the mother kills the father. In the second play, the son Orestes kills his mother to take revenge for his father. The hands of the gods are constantly present in the story: Artemis demands Iphigenia's death, and Orestes is guided by Apollo in killing his own mother.

This third play, the *Eumenides,* makes the role of the gods more explicit and brings the level of conflict to that of the gods. After killing his mother, Orestes is beset by the Furies, ancient goddesses born from the goddess Night. This goddess is one of the first generations of the gods, and so the Furies are of the same generation as the children of Gaia, who was the first goddess to possess Delphi. The Furies fulfill the duty of punishing any who murder their own blood. They drive the murderers over the face of the earth, tormenting them and eventually driving them mad. Near madness, Orestes flees to Delphi where the priests of Apollo cleanse him of the miasma of his action. Apollo himself declares him faultless. But the Furies do not depart or flee in the face of Apollo; instead, they reject his judgment and name him a thief:

Ah, son of Zeus! You are a thief!
Young as you are, you had ridden us down, aged divinities—
respecting the suppliant, a godless man,
hurtful to parents.
You have stolen away the matricide, god that you are!
What is there in this that any shall say is just?[19]

Here, on the stolen ground of Delphi, we have goddesses almost as old as the original keeper of the temple calling its new occupant a thief. Repeatedly throughout the play, the Furies insist that they are called to punish any who spill the blood of their kin.[20] When the Furies demand their right and challenge Apollo's authority, they risk reigniting a war over the throne of Olympus itself.

Apollo, fearful of starting a new war amongst the gods, takes Orestes along with the Furies to Athens to appeal to the wiser Athena. To address the standoff, Athena appeals to the idea of wisdom through council and invents the democratic court system. She calls in her citizens to make a judgment, and then she has Apollo, Orestes, and the Furies each state their case.

The case is about far more than the crime of Orestes; rather, it is about an older order of the cosmos versus the new order and the comparative importance of fathers and mothers. Apollo even argues that mothers do not share the blood of their children, and thus Orestes did not kill his own blood, because it is possible for a man to give birth alone (as demonstrated by Zeus giving birth to Athena himself). Of course, the Furies might have responded that the earth, Gaia, gave birth on her own without a male counter-part, as did their own mother Nux, or Night.

The fact that the people of Athens are torn between the two sides shows that the conflict amongst the gods also represents a living conflict amongst the people in terms of spheres of meaning and value. Athena breaks the tie by siding with her brother as a proxy for her own father Zeus, whom she claims to support in all things. The Furies become enraged and threaten to curse the earth and all upon it. Athena counters that the fact that The Furies won half the vote shows that the council respects both sides of the issue. More importantly, the vote showed respect for both divine orders: neither was insulted or rejected.

Thus, the nature of the council is to recognize and accept the plurality of

---

19 Aeschylus, *Eumenides,* lines 149–54.
20 We can't help but think, "As Kronos did to his father, as Zeus did to Kronos."

truth, even when all truths can't win at the same time and place. This alone does not satisfy the Furies. Athena must then promise them a place of honor in the courts of Athens, so that *their* sense of justice and *their* understanding of right and wrong will also have a place in the council and not be overruled by newer spheres of meaning.

The innovations found in the *Eumenides*, tying the establishment of democracy to the wars amongst the generations of the gods, may be built upon an earlier text—quite possibly the "Homeric Hymn to Hermes," which is from around 510 BC (pre-dating the *Eumenides* by about fifty years). The hymn tells the amusing story of the one day old Hermes getting into trouble and, by doing so, claiming his place on Olympus. Hermes is born in a cave on earth, a late-born illegitimate child of Zeus and the nymph Maia:

> And then she bore a child of many turns, crafty of counsel,
> a robber, a driver of cattle, a leader of dreams,
> a watcher at night, a thief at the gates, who would quickly
> reveal glorious deeds among the immortal gods.
> Born at dawn, at mid-day he played the lyre,
> In the evening he stole the cattle of far-shooting Apollo.[21]

There are two points about the story that are particularly interesting. First, it is through theft and lies that Hermes will work his way into being accepted in Olympus. Second, to win his place in Olympus Hermes must engage in a conflict with other gods. It is through conflict that a new order which includes Hermes comes about. This conflict could not, however, be a direct clash of powers, for such a confrontation would threaten the stability of Olympus itself. Instead, it will be a competition of wits and deception.

The newborn Hermes leaves the place of his birth and immediately invents the musical instrument the lyre. Then, he finds Apollo's cattle and steals them away, using a trick to conceal their footprints. Apollo soon finds Hermes and demands his cattle back, to which Hermes responds by saying he is a newborn baby and it is absurd to think he could steal cattle, whatever cattle may be. Apollo is not fooled, so the two go before Zeus for judgment. Before Zeus, once again Apollo offers his accusations and Hermes lies extensively to the entire assembly of the gods, an act that greatly impresses his father Zeus:

---

21 Susan Chadwick Shelmerdine, "Homeric Hymn to Hermes," *The Homeric Hymns* (Brantford, Ont.: W. Ross MacDonald School Resource Services Library, 2008), 13–18.

But Hermes told another story among the immortals
and explained to Kronios, leader of all the gods,
"Father Zeus, indeed I will tell you the truth,
for I am truthful and do not know how to lie..."
Zeus laughed loudly when he saw his mischievous son
making denials so well and skillfully about the cattle.[22]

Zeus rules that Hermes and Apollo must each go forth together and look for the cattle, and Hermes must guide the search in good faith. Hermes does indeed lead Apollo faithfully to the hidden cattle, and even Apollo marvels at the ingenuity of the clever child thief. Having fulfilled Zeus' order and impressed his father with his skilled deceptions, Hermes then wooes Apollo. He pulls out the lyre and begins playing and singing, and Apollo is transfixed:

Slayer of cattle, contriver of plots, hard worker, comrade of the feast,
these things you have invented are worth fifty cows.
And so I think we shall settle our differences peacefully hereafter...
For full of wonder is this newly-revealed sound I am hearing,
a sound which I say no one of men has ever yet learned
nor any of the immortals who have their homes on Olympus
far from you, thieving son of Zeus and Maia.
What skill, what music for inescapable cares,
what path? For surely one can take three things together in all:
joy and love and sweet sleep.[23]

Hermes offers to trade him the lyre for the cattle. Apollo agrees, which is how Apollo became the god of music and the lyre and Hermes became the god of cattle (and thieves and liars, amongst other things).

We see in these examples how deception, including re-naming or flattery, is a strategy to negotiate power, as well as to negotiate dangerous situations in which powers too great to be unleashed risk conflict with each other. There is a deeper point here when we take into account the two short quotations with which I started this interlude. Apollo, through the Oracle of Delphi, does not speak plainly or lie but rather gives a sign. Similarly, the Muses boast to Hesiod that they know how to tell the truth and how to lie—a rather disconcerting thing to be said to a mortal about to learn the nature of reality from these same talented truth-tellers and liars.

---

22 Shelmerdine, "Homeric Hymn to Hermes," 366–69, 389–90.
23 Shelmerdine, "Homeric Hymn to Hermes," 436–38, 443–49.

Deception is tied into the very nature of pagan divinity. Pagan myths throughout the world often reveal divine power to be as much about successful deception and transformation as it is about raw might. This last point concerning transformation gets to the real heart of the issue. As we saw in the case of the Furies, renaming can involve a process of transforming a dangerous and hostile force into a friendly and useful one. The Furies, when named the Eumenides, literally become a blessing to the people as a pillar of their justice system. A lie, when told by a god, can become the truth and transform what was. A lie, when told to a god and accepted, becomes a new reality.

It is for this reason that the Oracle at Delphi cannot simply tell the truth. The truth, in a pagan metaphysics, isn't a stable and singular thing that can be captured in direct speech. As the Pre-Socratic philosopher Heraclitus knew well, the ways of writing and speaking must be both crooked and straight to capture the pluralistic nature of all that is. Thus, reality is best captured through those brothers and sisters to the lie; riddles, puzzles, and paradox.

CHAPTER TWO
Cultures of the Story: On Orality & Literality

Understanding of the difference between an oral and literate culture is crucial for understanding the cultural and cognitive shifts caused by writing, as well as the conceptual blindness writing imposes upon our thought. Unfortunately, an inevitable historical chauvinism always accompanies us when we attempt to look "back" into oral cultures: an assumption that we are more advanced than our ancestors. When this assumption is combined with a good-hearted desire not to belittle ancient cultures, we often then arrive at the false conclusion that the ancients must have thought just like us, since concluding they thought differently must mean they thought worse.

Nothing can be further from the truth. Oral cultures think very differently, but they do not think worse than us. It is not historically accurate to assume that people without writing think the same way as people with writing. We are not talking about the difference between individuals, however: someone who is illiterate in contemporary New York City is still the product of a thoroughly literate culture. Every piece of the culture that forms a modern illiterate person is nevertheless informed by writing, even when they themselves can't read.

An oral culture and a literate culture are very different in terms of their engagement with the world and understanding of reality—a difference that is very hard for us to grasp. First let us be clear: stating that oral societies think differently from us is not to state they were less advanced or less complicated than us. They were *different*. There were some things they didn't think which we think. Some of the things we think that they do not distort our understanding of reality and prevent us from understanding theirs. There are some things they easily recognized and thought which we find extremely difficult to grasp.

Their thought was superior to ours in very specific ways; ours has strengths that theirs lacked.

We are dealing, in each case, with *difference* and not *superiority*. Set aside assumptions about the "progress" of history. Consider it in terms of the senses. To compare oral and literate societies in terms of superiority is to ask whether it would be better to be able only to hear without seeing or only see without hearing.

Though we cannot fully give up the "vision" we have because of writing, we might still be able to "hear" as our ancestors did and use this new sense to identify the failures of our "vision."

What is Seen and What is Heard

While language for us is largely understood as pattern made physical, for oral societies the nature of language is the echo and not the code. This point is made very nicely by Eric Havelock, one of the heroes of a true appreciation of orality:

> A communication system of this sort is an echo system, light as air and as fleeting. Yet we are given to describing its character and effects as though they were some kind of material existing in some kind of space. They become "patterns" and "codes" and "themes" and "monumental compositions." They have "content" and "substance." Their behavior becomes, linguistically speaking, a matter of "grammar," a term which by its very derivation betrays the source of its invention in the behavior of words as written, not spoken. Its rules are said to be 'imprinted' on our brains. If preserved, it becomes "information," which is "packaged" and "stored" in the warehouse of the mind. These metaphors and dozens like them are those of a literate culture which has long been used to looking at language as written, at that point where it ceases to be echo and becomes artifact.[24]

As Havelock makes clear, we understand the very nature of language and thought on the model of the written word, a model which obscures from us the nature of oral language and thinking. The visual nature of written language

---

24 Eric Alfred Havelock, *The Muse Learns to Write* (Yale University Press, 1986), 66. For further reading on the topic of orality and its influence upon thought a good start would be Havelock, *Preface to Plato*; Walter Ong, *Orality and Literacy*; Kevin Robb, *Language and Thought in Early Greek Philosophy*.

shapes our views of knowledge as well, such that many of our metaphors for truth, fact, and understanding derive from forms of vision. Seeing becomes the basis for believing, and undermines other models of what it is to know and understand. Consider as simple an example as our use of the term "clarity." I hope this book and its argument will be clear, and this desired clarity in thought and argumentation is derived from vision: being able to see something without obstruction or distortion.[25]

Visual metaphors for truth prioritize singularity. When we look at several things at once we either find that we cannot focus, or that some things stand in front of others and block each other from view. On the other hand, we can hear many sounds at once, enjoy multiple levels of music, and not necessarily suffer from cacophony.

The idea of unity found in visual literary cultures and oral auditory cultures differs. What it is for a visual object to be *one* is very different from the type of unity found in, say, a symphony. For example, visual unity relies entirely on spatiality, while auditory unity depends on time. Heraclitus will push other metaphors for knowledge and understanding beyond even this contrast between the visual and acoustic, noting that even were everything to turn into visually indiscernible smoke, still the nose would be able to distinguish between many things.

When we offer visual models of knowledge we also adopt the distance that vision implies and requires. We must have a certain ideal distance from things to see them. Knowledge modeled on vision requires just the right distance and separation from the thing in question. This is a basis of "objectivity" and the idea of neutral rationality. On the other hand, to have a taste for something, to feel something out, to understand in metaphors not based on vision, is often to be in contact with something. What we smell, touch, and taste is all about us and often enough within us. To understand, to have a knowledge modeled on taste and smell, is to allow the thing we would know to become part of us and enter into us.

---

25 Much can be learned, in fact, from the etymology of the word "clear." It comes from the Latin word *clarus* that had the basic meaning of shining and thus relies on a visual image. However, its older root in Indo-European which derives from an oral period of history instead ties the word into the verb "to call or shout" and provide a path for understanding *clarus* as "renown" or "well-spoken-of."

Prioritized Speech
Within Oral and Written Languages

The difference between oral thought and literate thought is greater than just the limitation of metaphors for knowledge, understanding, and truth. To make the real difference clearer, let's attempt to walk back out of a literate world and into an oral one. We tend to think of language as primarily used for personal communication between individuals. This is hardly its most important social function, however. Language is ultimately a tool of memory, a tool that captures and maintains what a community learns over time. Language allows us to pass learning from generation to generation and from community to community. Historically, the most important role of language has been its role in remembering and preserving. Written language does this by default, but societies without written language must wage a constant battle against forgetting.

Every society has distinctions between different types of language. The most basic of these is a distinction between the socially prioritized language that preserves and embodies tradition (as well as the authority of that tradition), and the common language of everyday speech. We can see this difference in the type of language we use in speeches, written laws, and formal documents, versus the way we might speak to our friends. For a starker contrast, consider the role of Latin throughout medieval and early modern Europe. Latin was the language of law, scholarship, and religion, versus the local languages such as French, German, or English. Something similar was the case with Mandarin in China. More than dialects or languages being privileged as carriers of preserved traditional knowledge and official political power, the written word becomes the privileged form of language for all official communication.

Social power and class distinctions are built into and upon these distinctions. Consider how one sign of an "educated" individual is the ability to write differently than they speak. Use of slang and dialect in writing breaks the standards of privileged preserved speech. The racist and classist aspects of this system are apparent: writing closer to the way one actually talks marks the writer as "uneducated," and thus their words are given less weight.

The prioritized speech within written (as opposed to oral) languages is often molded overtly for technical clarity (thus the precision of legalese). It is also covertly structured to special initiation (i.e., the education and technical training necessary to understand and craft legalese). That special initiation allows certain classes to maintain power over prioritized language. This gate-keeping aspect of prioritized language will appear in one form or another in any cultural context, but the written word's commitment to technical clarity is not shared with oral language.

While clarity is of primary importance for literate cultures, memorability is important to oral cultures. Prioritized speech in an oral culture is built to be able to be memorized and passed on with a minimum of change from one person and generation to another. This is almost the exact opposite of legal-ese; with its mind-numbing technicalities, it is exceptionally hard to memorize or pass it on in any form other than writing.

The Worldview of Oral Cultures

To understand the worldview and psychology of an oral culture we need only ask what type of speech is most memorable, easy to pass on to future gener-ations, and likely to maintain a high degree of accuracy over long periods of time. Researchers on orality have approached this work in three ways. First, they have investigated surviving oral cultures for the key characteristics those cultures and their mode of speech display. Representative of this type of work was the ethnographic study of Serbian oral epic poetry performed by Milman Parry and Albert Lord in the 1920s. These studies led to the recognition that the so-called works of Homer are in fact written records of previously oral works passed down for many generations before the development of writing in Greece. Second, researchers have studied the structures of works we now know were originally oral such as *Beowulf*, the Homeric epics, parts of the Hebrew Bible, many of the Hindu Vedas (in particular the *Rig Veda*), and so on. Third, investigations of early written works composed at the end of an oral culture and beginning of a literary one allow us to capture the conceptual, lin-guistic, and psychological changes that the use of writing imposes. The repre-sentative examples here are studies of Pre-Socratic and Platonic philosophy, as well as early Classical Greek literature

These three avenues of study have confirmed several points about oral privi-leged speech. To be memorable, speech presents ideas in terms of action and concrete scenarios; in other words, in terms of active narratives. "Tradition in short is taught by action, and not by idea or principle."[26] These narratives are

---

26 Havelock, *The Muse Learns to Write*, 77.

presented in audible forms that lend themselves to memorization with rhythm, meter, rhyme, changes in pitch, and so on. Prioritized speech in an oral culture is poetry that was generally sung, often accompanied with music and dancing. Some of these points are stressed by Havelock in a very useful passage:

> A language of action rather than reflection appears to be a prerequisite for oral memorization... The more fundamental fact of his linguistic operation is that all subjects of statements have to be narrativised, that is, they must be names of agents who do things, whether actual persons or other forces which are personified. The predicates to which they attach themselves must be predicates of action or of situation present in action, never of essence or existence.[27]

The statement about essence and existence is very important and points to the larger aspect of oral culture: they do not have abstract concepts, but rather think in terms of concrete particulars. There are *good people*, for example, and if you ask about what is *good* you will be given examples from poetry of specific people performing specific good actions, but there is no concept of *goodness* in general. A mode of thinking founded in active narrative captures general principles through paradigmatic or archetypal examples, not through a grasp of general, universal, abstract characteristics.

Narrative scenes form a web or lace of meanings. Remembering and understanding these multiple meanings is how to understand any given thing. To know *goodness* is to know as many examples as possible and to be able to relate these examples to each other. In other words, an oral culture is pluralistic and non-reductive at its very conceptual, linguistic, and psychological basis. A literary culture, on the other hand, understands meaning and the nature of a thing in terms of one ultimate or general reductive meaning.[28]

We can understand this web or fabric of meanings better when we notice that *oral thought* has the same structure as *oral performance*. The auditory structure of poetry is paralleled by a conceptual or "semantic" structure. Images and ideas echo each other, setting up patterns of imagistic and thematic repetitions. The introduction of a new idea is achieved through echoing and variation of previous ideas and themes. From Havelock again: "This something new must occur as a partial echo of something already said: It is a

---

27 Havelock, *The Muse Learns to Write*, 76.
28 The points made in Chapter One concerning differences in the understanding of definition (between an essentialist definition and one based more on family resemblance) are therefore actually points about the contrast between a literate and oral culture.

'difference contained within the same,' the 'same' being the metrical beat or the thematic resemblance."[29]

This echoing and semantic rhythm gives rise to the most basic nature of oral thought and language: parataxis. Parataxis is a poetic form of listing where no item in the list is given priority.[30] Oral speech and thought are additive, they follow an associative logic in which one thing is added to another to create larger more complex situations or ideas. This is the logic of "and, also" instead of "either, or." Different ideas are built up out of resemblances; no reduction to a prioritized meaning or message is possible. In parataxis, there is no structure of subordination: each element is as important and meaningful as the others. Each element adds to the multiplying and increasingly complex plethora of meanings available. Parataxis is the logic of pluralism, rather than monism or holism, and it is a logic and method of thinking where totalization and reduction are absent.

The Temporal and The Many

This absence of reductive general meaning, this lack of abstract conceptualization, means that the thinking of oral cultures focuses on the particular and specific. Oral culture is refreshingly concrete and worldly, without the transcendental thinking that tries to leap beyond the boundaries of the world into abstract concepts of perfection and goodness. Consider our concepts of the infinite and eternal, both abstract concepts impossible to grasp in a concrete way. In oral cultures, gods are not eternal or infinite, (indeed it is unclear what these things could even mean); instead, gods are without-limit and undying and ever-living. In fact, as we will discuss in a later chapter, even gods die frequently enough, and "ever-living" is more a description of a state than an eternal truth or promise.

---

29 Havelock, *The Muse Learns to Write*, 73.

30 The most famous example of parataxis is probably the statement attributed to Julius Caesar: "I came; I saw; I conquered." Another famous example can be found in 1 Corinthians 13:4: "Love is patient, love is kind. It does not envy, it does not boast, it is not proud. It does not dishonor others, it is not self-seeking, it is not easily angered, it keeps no record of wrongs." A third example is the striking opening of Dicken's *A Tale of Two Cities*: "It was the best of times, it was the worst of times, it was the age of wisdom, it was the age of foolishness, it was the epoch of belief, it was the epoch of incredulity, it was the season of Light, it was the season of Darkness, it was the spring of hope, it was the winter of despair, we had everything before us, we had nothing before us, we were all going direct to Heaven, we were all going direct the other way."

The point about the difference between eternal/infinite and immortal/ever-living overlaps with the difference between a visual model of unity and an auditory model. Auditory thinking is based on time instead of space, while visuality prioritizes space and distance.

In a visual model of unity, concepts such as the infinite or eternal are presented in terms of something spatially singular, despite the fact that they are also concepts of time. So, the infinite or the eternal are understood as things which do not pass through time (therefore, unchanging) or as something that is co-extensive with space (therefore, universal). In other words, visual unity performs a translation of temporality into space.

On the other hand, auditory unity allows for a thinking that is based through and through on time. There can be no narrative thought or understanding in terms of active agents without time as a basis. This focus on time at the foundation of oral thinking means that the cosmos of oral societies is one without transcendental, abstract, unchanging laws.

Eros or sexual desire is one of the foundations of the Greek world, driving all things on to change, grow, bring about the new, and fade from existence. Eros is also a reflection of the unending drive of time and change which rest at the basis of the cosmos, in which there are no unchanging structures. As Heraclitus, an early user of written language who still captures the oral worldview, is said to have put it: *all things flow*. Cultures of speech, of narrative, of poetry—that is oral cultures, high pagan cultures—are cultures of the inevitability of change.[31]

The Conflict Between Oral and Written Thought

The difference between an oral and literate culture (and their different modes of thought) is one reason why Socrates' questions regarding the nature of virtue are so often met with confusion by his interlocutors. The people with whom he spoke weren't idiots; their oral mode of thought and the metaphysics embodied in it did not reduce distinct individual realities to abstract entities such as "Goodness in-itself by-itself."

---

31   This focus on change goes along with an understanding of all things as forces, personalities, and moving active agencies, a key aspect of most forms of animism. The animism of pagan cultures, which we will discuss much more extensively in a later chapter, is a central aspect of oral cultures.

48

Socrates: Come then, let us examine what we mean. An action or a man dear to the gods is pious, but an action or a man hated by the gods is impious. They are not the same, but quite opposite, the pious and the impious. Is that not so?
Euthyphro: It is indeed.
Socrates: And that seems to be a good statement?
Euthyphro: I think so, Socrates.
Socrates: We have also stated that the gods are in a state of discord, that they are at odds with each other, Euthyphro, and that they are at enmity with each other. Has that, too, been said?[32]

The Platonic dialogue *Euthyphro* explores the nature of goodness under the heading of "piety" and its relation to the gods. Socrates insists that if we are going to arrive at a unified understanding of the Good, or the version of it found in piety, we are going to have to reject the multiplicity of the gods. With multiple gods there can be no singular definition of piety, or ultimately virtue and goodness.

Plato is pushing his own agenda in the dialogues, one that consists of a rejection of the gods of archaic poetry and myth in favor of eternal, perfect, inhuman, and unchanging divine principles. For this reason, we should not be surprised to find Socrates' debate partners so willing to give ground on the abstract unity of goodness. One might wish Euthyphro himself were just a bit smarter and were, to put it bluntly, *a bit more Greek*. Then he might have asked "Why precisely should I be concerned to come up with a unifying general definition of piety or goodness? What makes this necessary? May not 'good' or 'pious' be meant in many senses — senses derived from many and different gods?"

Alas, we do not get this dialogue, but it would have been one that captured better the nature of oral thought and of pagan thought. Despite that, in their repeated attempts to define things in terms of concrete narrative examples rather than the abstract universal concepts, Socrates' interlocutors attest to the difficulties the older oral culture's way of thinking encountered against the thinking informed by the written word that usurped it.

Rationality derived from writing and reading relies on a cognitive and epistemic distance based on visual models of knowledge. It is also objectifying. You can begin to see this point more clearly if you think about the difference

---

32 Plato, G. M. A. Grube, and John M. Cooper, *The Trial and Death of Socrates: Euthyphro, Apology, Crito, Death Scene from Phaedo* (Indianapolis, IN: Hackett Pub., 1975).

between the spoken and written word. To hear the spoken word, to bene-fit from its knowledge, one must be present with the speaker. On the other hand, writing turns the content of the speech into an independent, stable ob-ject seemingly existing without an anchor in time, place, or speaker. Written words "speak" independent of their origin; they thus appear to have an ab-stract neutrality and objectivity. At the same time, they move the object of their "speech" to a similarly abstract objective space, creating an unavoidable distance between the reader/writer/thinker and the object.

Poetic performance, on the other hand, was understood to bring its object to appearance. Song evokes—summons forth—the object of the song, and places the listener in contact with it.

This objectifying nature of the thought of a literate society shows up in many of our very worst modern characteristics. It also runs deeply throughout mono-theistic metaphysics. The monotheistic god is most often an abstract goodness or perfection, a strange monster impossible to grasp in an active, concrete, associative logic. This god's "goodness" seems to have no consequences for the actual pain and struggles of those around us in the world.

I often make this point for my students by asking, in concrete terms, what dif-ference the existence or nonexistence of the monotheistic, perfect god would make for the world around us. In other words, what would you predict to never see if such a god exists, and what would you predict to see as evidence if it did? Could we say, for example, that innocent children would never suffer and die of cancer if such a good god existed?

The answer for most believers is clearly "no." Instead, "god works in strange and mysterious ways," which is a dodge allowing absolutely any worldly re-alities to be consistent with a god whose "goodness" is removed from life. If the one god were good, we could have this world; if it were evil, we could have this same world; if it didn't exist at all, we could have this same world again. Thus, "goodness" here is clearly a word without concrete content.

From the standpoint of the one ultimate creator-god, the world or the uni-verse is an object. It is an artifact with purpose, intended for use. This basic perspective filters down to all aspects of reality: all things are able to be reduced to objects for use. The human repeats the stance of the one god, seeing earth, animal, plant, and even each other as objects reducible to raw material and use.

As touched upon in our earlier discussion of definitions, within a monothe-istic culture built upon thought structured through writing, a thing's nature or essence is timeless and unchanging. Sometimes this is understood to be its essence as held in the mind of god, or its purpose as intended from the beginning of time. Since the monotheistic god is timeless, so too are the ultimate natures of all things. On the other hand, the parataxic nature of oral thinking (its associative logic of "and, also") sees a thing's nature as changing over time, consisting of the many increasing relationships it has with all other things. What a thing *is* involves the resonances it holds with the rest of the cosmos, its place in the web. Those echoes and resonances shift. We are in-touch with things, interpenetrated and interpenetrating.

The conceptual frameworks of oral societies do not contain abstract general universal elements. This means that their view of individual things does not reduce them to general essences, but rather builds things up out of increasingly complex associations and relations. This also means that the cosmos cannot be understood as reducible to one ultimate basis, because this basis or origin would be abstract. Instead, oral concepts are based on irreducible complexity in the form of parataxis, in which echoes and resonances relate to each other without any point in the web being able to be absolutely prioritized.

Oral cultures are pluralistic at their logical, linguistic, conceptual, and psychological basis. They also do not entertain that most abstract of concepts, the god outside of time and space, the god beyond existence, the transcendent god. Instead, things become understood in terms of *this* world, in terms of concrete and active realities. This also forecloses the thought of humans as separable from the rest of the world around them; in fact, nothing is conceivable as an isolated object. The body is not a prison and the earth is not a testing ground for some higher timeless purpose. This is a world of connections, echoes, dependencies, resonances and not of absolutely individual things.

As can be seen from this, many of the concepts of pagan metaphysics and theology are also the basic aspects of an oral culture. For this reason it can uncontroversially be said that, using the sense of the word pagan developed earlier in this book, oral cultures have always and everywhere been primarily pagan.

SECOND INTERLUDE
The Wisdom of Multiple Meanings

Obanyansofoo yebu no be, yennka no asem.
"The wise is spoken to in proverbs, not plain language."[33]

A central aspect of meaning in oral societies is its irreducibility to one meaning, and we see this web of echoing resonances clearest in the attitude of most oral societies towards proverbs. To speak well, in oral Archaic and later Classical Greece, was to speak through heavy references to traditional sayings and proverbs. The model of a good speech was one built upon the bones of heavy quotation. To speak well, which also meant to speak wisely and to speak the truth, was to speak in the manner of the prioritized speech of the oral tradition, to speak with the very words, phrases, and sayings of the already established tradition.

The same precise characteristic exists in the traditional Akan society in Ghana, as discussed by Kwasi Wiredu: "Beautiful speech is one that develops a coherent and persuasive argument, clinching points—and this is crucial— with striking and decisive proverbs. Anybody not possessed of such a tongue can forget any ambitions of high office."[34] This same characteristic can be found in many Native American cultures as well as those of the Norse, as attested to by the *Havamal*. *Havamal* is a poem presenting a series of wisdom sayings in the voice of Odin, many of which clearly represent older oral and traditional proverbs. Consider the following selections from the *Havamal*:

---

33 Traditional Akan proverb
34 Wiredu, *Cultural Universals and Particulars*, 62.

A better burden can no man bear
on the way than his mother wit.[35]

A bird of Unmindfulness flutters o'er ale feast.[36]

A coward believes he will ever live
if he keep him safe from strife:
but old age leaves him not long in peace
though spears may spare his life.[37]

The miserable man and evil minded
makes of all things mockery.[38]

The proverbs of oral cultures are not as straightforward as they seem, however, as Wiredu frequently points out in regard to Akan sayings. Whereas we tend to break down a proverb into one meaning, oral proverbs do not in fact have singular meanings. They are a repository of wisdom, a collection of multiple meanings, many of them inconsistent with others. Proverbs can be used in opposite situations from one moment to the next, used to support one course of action at one time and shifting to support another at another time.

A good starting example of these multiple meanings is one of the famous mottoes of the Oracle of Delphi, *gnothi seauton* or, "know thyself." This has variously been understood to mean: one should not boast but rather focus on one's own weaknesses and failures, the gods dwell within us and we should look within to understand divinity, the gods aren't worth thinking about and one should instead make humanity the basis of one's studies, one should recognize that one is ignorant, and many other meanings. Clearly some of these meanings are complimentary, others are overtly contradictory.

This multiplicity distinguishes a saying such as "Know thyself" from something like a guiding ethical principle or rule of thumb. Proverbs are not principles, because principles have one reductive meaning that can be applied consistently to different cases. Indeed, the multiple and often contradictory meanings of proverbs directs us to a model of knowledge and wisdom entirely foreign to most contemporary modes of thought. Unlike paradoxes,

---

35 Olive Bray and W. G. Collingwood, *The Poetic Edda: Illustrated - Original Text with English Translation - including a Glossary of Terms* (Brighton, Vic.: Leaves of Gold Press, 2013), 11.

36 Bray, *The Poetic Edda*, 13.

37 Bray, *The Poetic Edda*, 16.

38 Bray, *The Poetic Edda*, 22.

unlike riddles, in proverbs there is no solution but rather an ever-growing web of wise and changing messages.

This sort of thinking is similar and parallel to many approaches to Tarot and most forms of divination. Though at the beginning one learns set "meanings" for each card in Tarot, these set meanings become inadequate when one approaches true ability with the cards. Each card has many meanings, and many of these meanings are contradictory. The art of reading the cards requires understanding how the full cards in a spread constitute a web of meanings that are mutually interpretive. Each card tells us how the others are to be read, along with the card's position in the spread. On top of this, a truly skilled reader will also be able to feel out which of the many possible meanings fits best with the querent and the general situation, question, or concern being addressed.

Let us look at a few more examples from the Greek context before looking a bit more widely at other examples from pagan cultures. Greek culture had a collection of proverbs attributed to Thales, a Pre-Socratic philosopher from whom we have no extant texts but who became a symbol of the "wise man" in general in Greece. Sayings attributed to Thales are particularly interesting because they tend to capture very well the art of multiple meanings. For example, "What is easy? To advise another." This can mean, alternatively, that it is very easy to offer advice but much harder to actually aid someone or to follow advice on your own part. It can also mean that to advise another is a good and easy thing that we should do. One could imagine being told this saying in a case where we are offering pompous advice to someone, and also being told this saying when we are unsure how to help a friend and are being encouraged to offer them advice.

Here is another of Thales' proverbs: "What is the strangest thing? An aged tyrant." Again, two immediate meanings jump to mind. Either: tyrants are prone to being killed young and therefore usually don't live to old age; or, alternatively, that the aged are more likely to recognize the evil of tyranny and refuse to have any part of it. A third possible meaning is that the young are more naturally tyrannical, that there is something about the spiritedness of youth that drives it to dominate.[39]

The multi-leveled and pluralistic nature of proverbs reflects a similar characteristic of certain types of myth, where lessons about the nature of reality

---

39   The idea that there is something naturally tyrannical about youth would be a fairly standard Greek insight into the role of unbridled passion and spirit in the formation of a tyrant.

are often able to be derived in dramatically different ways. A third of the famous sayings of Thales can serve to clarify this point. "What is most common? Hope. Because even to those who have nothing else it is nearby." This is a clear reflection of one version of the legend of Pandora's box. When Pandora opened the box all the evils of human life were released upon the world, but within the box one thing alone remained: hope.

For years I struggled with what this was intended to mean. The common reading is that with evil came hope as well, as a sort of cure or at least solace. This is certainly one interpretation but it ignores the details of the myth. Hope is not released into the world, it remains in the box. This could mean, in a very tragic sense that would resonate with Greek culture, that hope does not exist in human life: it rests still locked away in Pandora's box. I believe that both meanings are intended, the contradictory meanings each forming the web of the full meaning of the myth.

The same contradiction resonates in Thales' proverb. The idea of something being "common" in Greek is not normally one with a positive connotation. For hope to be common could also mean that it is cheap and worthless. This interpretation is reinforced in the second half of the proverb, when hope is identified as the possession of the poor as well as the rich. Though the full resonance does not necessarily remain for contemporary readers, there is a distinct tone of dismissal present here. So, although one meaning—and certainly an intended one—is that when all else is lost we always have hope, it also implies that hope is not of great value. Again, one could imagine hearing this saying both when in a situation of desperation and when being scolded for being overly optimistic.

Ancient myth and modern divination both offer models of the multiple meanings of proverbs, but there is a related ancient example that we are also familiar with: the unique art forms of oracle and prophecy. It is common to think of prophecy as riddling, hiding meaning that only becomes clear later. In this regard, the famous Oracle of Delphi is a good example. However, seeing only the riddle without its deeper nature is to miss an important point. Riddles have singular answers, but oracles, in connecting with the multiple irreducible nature of reality and the future, instead have multiple possible meanings precisely because of the pluralistic nature of reality.

Nowhere is this multiple meaning of an oracle more obvious on the surface than in the story of Croesus. Croesus was the king of Lydia; during the rise of the Persian Empire he was the last major defense of the Ionian Greek cities against the Persian Empire. Croesus sent a delegate to Delphi to ask whether he should attack the Persian Empire and was told that if he attacked the Persians "he would destroy a great empire." He thought that was a good omen and attacked, only to be defeated and captured by the Persians. This constituted the end of Croesus' Lydian empire, famed for its amazing wealth. However, it is not that the oracle was really saying that Croesus would destroy his own empire if he attacked, it is that the future cast by the oracle was multiple, and all its various meanings and possibilities were existed until one became manifest.

We can see a clearer case of this in the oracle offered to a friend of Socrates who asked if anyone was wiser than Socrates. The oracle stated that no man was wiser than Socrates. Socrates himself argued, in his defense before the court of Athens, that this couldn't possibly mean that he was actually wise, because he claimed to know nothing. Instead: true wisdom meant recognizing that human wisdom was equally worthless compared to the wisdom of the gods.

This is clearly one meaning of the oracle; another is suggested but not claimed by Socrates, that wisdom consists in the recognition of ignorance and the pursuit of learning. Yet another meaning is also likely meant, that Socrates was indeed a very wise person. Thus, the oracle means both that Socrates was and wasn't wise, and also that human wisdom is and isn't worth pursuing.

One final example of this type of oracle may be useful. When the Persians were invading Greece, the Athenians sent a delegation to Delphi to ask what should be done. Eventually, and with reluctance, the oracle told the Athenians to "let your wooden walls defend you." This answer was deeply mysterious, for Athens had stone walls. Some argued that the people should hide in the Parthenon because it had once had wooden walls. Others argued that Athens had ships with wooden walls. Eventually, Athens fought the Persians at sea, a truly brilliant military move (the Athenians had a skilled navy and the Persians were much more adept at warfare on land). This led to the resounding defeat of the Persians and the freeing of Greece from Persian rule. However, we don't know what the history of the alternative path might have been. On the surface, it seems a terrible military strategy to hide in a temple, but oracles have a strange way of working out.

If speaking well means speaking in well-chosen and well-presented proverbs, this tells us something about what it is to be wise. Since the art of speech is also an art of understanding the multiple meanings of proverbs (and understanding the multiple imports of a given situation in order to apply a proverb), wisdom involves a recognition of the pluralism of reality. Using and understanding proverbs well requires recognizing the associative and contradictory nature of existence. In other words, to use proverbs well is to be able to read the world itself as a proverb. This is the same art involved in divination and oracle, and also the understanding of myth. To understand is to see the multiple without reducing it to the singular or universal.

Proverbs thus point to an art of understanding both language and the world, and we can see this in one of the defining characteristics of the Spartans. The Spartans were famous for several things, including their military prowess and their horrific slave-state, but also for their tendency to say a lot in very few words.[40] Greek history is full of delightful examples of the Spartan style of speech; unfortunately, this style is inevitably understood from the wrong end. Before the laconic style became a manner of speech, it was first a way of understanding the words of others. In fact, all the best examples of Spartan speech derive from a clever understanding of words spoken to a Spartan, with the response playing on the multiple and ambiguous meanings of the words. That is, instead of being a manner of speech, it is a manner of listening. This characteristic of Spartan thought is based in the exceptionally conservative and religious nature (by Greek standards) of Spartan culture. The Spartans were particularly obsessed with oracles, omens, and signs whose understanding involved the pluralistic understanding of meaning.

I will offer the three best and most well-known examples of Spartan speech to make this point clear. First: Spartan wives and mothers supposedly told their sons and husbands when they left for war to "return carrying your shield or upon it." While there is really only one clear meaning for this statement, it is based upon the multiple levels of meaning involved in the shields carried by Spartan fighters. The Spartans favored large shields that were too heavy to run with. Also, when a warrior fell in battle they would be carried home upon their large shield. Thus, someone returning without his shield must have run during battle, and thus left his shield behind. So, the fact that the shield represented protection, one's deathbed, and a thing that couldn't be carried in retreat grants this saying its meaning: *die rather than flee.*

A second story about Sparta involves the Persian invasion of Greece. Leonidas, one of the kings of Sparta, marched off to delay the Persian invasion

---

40 In fact, our word "laconic," meaning using few words, derives from the name of the Spartan state, Lacodaemonia.

of Greece by making a fatal stand at Thermopylae.[41] On the way, he was told that there were so many Persians that their arrows blocked out the sun. His response was simply, "then we shall fight in the shade." This is clearly a striking example of bravado, but it also plays on the very simple distinction between a statement's literal meaning and intended affect.

My favorite example of the laconic art of listening involves the invasion of Greece by the forces of Philip II of Macedonia, Alexander the Great's father. Philip sent a message to Sparta as his forces sought to conquer Greece which read: "You are advised to submit without further delay, for if I bring my army into your land, I will destroy your farms, slay your people, and raze your city." The response sent by the Spartans consisted of one word, a word that made clear they had read the message in all its levels of meaning and hit upon the one point of weakness that reflected a similar weakness in Philip. The Spartan response was: "If."

This laconic art of understanding and speech can be found in many pagan cultures, including several Native American cultures. For now, however, I want to shift to considering a slightly different example of proverbial wisdom: the role of lists and especially triads in Celtic wisdom.[42] The list format of much of the oldest Celtic wisdom, for example in the "Thirteen Treasures of the Island of Britain," "Three Fair Princes of the Island of Britain," or "Three Fortunate Concealments of the Island of Britain," attests to the paratactic and associative logic of an oral tradition.

Celtic triads evince the same non-hierarchical listing (paratactic) aspect of oral thought captured beautifully in the practice of Homeric simile in Greece, in which the resonance between one image and an event give deeper meaning to both things, as when waves are described as horses and warriors are described as bees. For example, consider the following triads:

---

41 Sparta maintained two kings so that one could go off to battle without leaving the city unruled.

42 The dating and provenance of the so-called Celtic or Druidic Triads is a difficult matter, and we find particularly clear examples of them in both Ireland and Wales. They are largely derived from medieval texts mostly written by Christian monks recording older traditions. Some of them have been preserved, as well, through folk tradition. Perhaps the clearest example of them comes from the *Trioedd Ynys Prydein* which is itself a collection of various medieval manuscripts, or selections from such manuscripts, primarily from the thirteenth and fourteenth century including *The White book of Rhydderch and The Red book of Hergest*. Recently, new triads have also been invented and added to the collected wisdom.

Three things not easy to stop: the stream of a cataract, an arrow from a bow, and a rash tongue.

Three things very like each other: an old blind horse playing the harp with his hoofs, a pig in silk dress, a merciless person lecturing about piety.

In both of these cases, as in Homeric simile, the analogy between natural and human behaviors enriches the meaning of both. However, wisdom triads present a striking model of multiple and contradictory meanings captured through three overt meanings. Perhaps the clearest of these runs as follows:

Three things a person is: what they think they are, what others think they are, what they really are.

In this triad, we see a highly-developed art of multiple, ambiguous, and contradictory meanings maintained at the same time. We are what we think we are, what others think we are, and what we "really" are all at the same time even—and especially—when these are not the same thing. This tension is heightened all the more by calling into question what could possibly be meant by "what we really are," after we are already told that what we really are is also what we think we are and others think we are. To reduce this triad to any one or two of the elements is to miss the point, as it would also be to come up with some clever meaning that does away with the tensions. The force of the triad is captured, in many cases, by asking a question and giving three different answers, each of which make sense but in a different context or way. We get multiple and irreducible answers. Sometimes these answers are supposed to set up resonances, and sometimes—as in the case of "what a person is"—they instead war with each other in irresolvable tensions.

Here is another example, this time of a triad that depends on resonance while, at the same time, calling each aspect into question through that resonance:

Three powerful things in the world: a ruler, a fool, the void.

In this triad, we can't look at any particular listed item without noticing the way it calls the others into question. If a fool can be powerful, how does that not undermine or question the concept of a ruler? Are we to understand a ruler to be akin to a fool? This tension becomes all the worse when we consider "the void." Is there some sense in which both fool and ruler partake of the void? Unlike the earlier case of "what a person really is," these triads depending on ambiguous resonances which attempt to present multiple contradictory irreducible truths while also using each truth to call into question the others. There is an instability here, a motion of thought, neither seeking nor achieving resolution.

While our contemporary thought tends to aim at consolidation, reduction, and thus finite clear conclusions, the thinking of a pagan culture aims at provocation. We are driven to think, driven to continually expand the web of our thinking and grasp of reality, reaching ever further into the resonances and multiplicities of meaning and truth. To once more dwell upon the provocative words of Heraclitus, a thinker who made the art of multiple meanings his expertise, proverbs are like oracles and myths and, "the god whose oracle is at Delphi neither speaks plainly nor conceals, but gives a sign."[43]

---

43 Heraclitus and T.M. Robinson. *Fragments* (Toronto: Univ. of Toronto Press, 1987), fragment 93.

CHAPTER THREE
All Things Living, A Pagan Animism

Our modern thinking is heavily structured by conceptual and philo-sophical innovations that became possible with the rise of writing and, more specifically, the grasp of abstraction. These led, eventu-ally, to the dominance of monotheism. In this regard, it is useful to note that the oldest parts of the Hebrew Bible that preserve oral traditions are largely pagan, albeit prioritizing one particular god, while those most influenced by writing begin to stress a conceptual metaphysical monotheism.

Amongst the distinctions created through abstraction is the exceptionally vexed distinction between nature and the supernatural or artificial, between the worldly and otherworldly, between body and mind/soul, and the distinction between the mundane and the transcendental. One final distinction, exception-ally simple and yet strikingly important, was nonexistent in the high pagan oral culture: the distinction between the living and nonliving. The concept of life in pagan culture is tied indivisibly with the concept of nature and that of divinity. Thrown into the mix is also the surprisingly challenging concept of "body."

Pagan Concepts of Nature and Spirit

Our later concept of nature being structured through balance and law make it possible to talk about nature as a stable order. The Ancient Greek concept of nature, on the other hand, derives from the process of *growing*. In oral Ar-chaic Greek (as preserved in Homer), there is no noun for "nature" but only a verbal form. The equivalent in English would be having "naturing" but no word for "nature." In Archaic Greek, the term is *phuo*, and it roughly means "to bring forth or produce." In fact, the history of the term "nature" is much the same, deriving from the Latin verb *nasci*, "to be born." For the Romans (who thought in Latin), nature is what is born and bears future generations. Similarly, in Greek, there is a general activity of bringing forth and producing, which later becomes the noun *phusis* which became translated into Latin as *natura*.

I am stressing the origin of concepts of nature because it shows why anything like a non-living nature would be literally unthinkable for the Ancient Greeks, especially the high pagan oral Greeks. This would also be rather foreign to the Romans for much of their history. We also see something similar in most other pagan oral cultures, as well.

Phusis as "that which produces" captures the full nature of the cosmos, a point made particularly clear when we think back to the reproductive understanding of the creation of the cosmos offered by Hesiod. In that story, the various aspects of the world around us are each understood as the living children of previous gods, from streams and mountains to oceans and the misty vapors of the skies. This force of production, however, is one that constantly changes the boundaries of what exists and is possible. Cosmos as a flourishing crowd of living beings is not open to unchanging order or firm law: all things change, and changes can only be postponed temporarily or channeled in various directions, not prevented. To put it bluntly, nature is all that is living and changing and this applies to everything that exists.

Our earliest concepts of nature are indivisible from the idea that nature is living. If we turn to consider the concepts of "life," we find another path that will be useful for our understanding of what we might call pagan animism. The pagan Greeks had three main words for life: *bios*, *zoe*, and *psyche*. These weren't necessarily distinctions amongst types of life as much as they delimited different aspects of the phenomenon of life. *Bios* applies to individual lives, such as "my way of life" or "the life of a dog" or "the political life." *Zoe* represents life in general, and reflections on the nature of the living such as we find in biology would be formulated in terms of *zoe*.

Most important for our purposes is the noun *psyche*. *Psyche* will eventually come to mean mind and/or soul (frequently there is no distinction between mind or soul in Greek thought, for example in the thought of Plato). This is the word from which we get the term "psychology," as well as an idea we will be discussing shortly, namely that of panpsychism. Originally, however, the term *psyche* was derived from terms for "breath"; in Homer, the term *psyche* primarily means "the breath of life." This breath can survive without the body:

it is a body within a body, and it is what grants a living thing its ability to grow and change. In Latin, the term that was understood to be the compliment or translation of *psyche* was another term for life that shares *psyche*'s specific origin. *anima*, meaning life as well as mind, comes from earlier terms for breath and even for wind or breeze.[44]

Our investigation of these interconnected concepts of life, from *phusis* to *anima*, has provided us with something of a paradox. *Phusis* is the original concept of nature and of cosmos, understood as made up of living things. Once we move to *psyche* and *anima* however, we find life identified with something that can separate from the body and provides a basis of making distinctions between living and dead. The paradox is, how do we understand death in a cosmos where everything is understood as living?

Heraclitus & Transformation

One path to an answer leads along the role played by breath and breeze in these tightly interwoven ideas. The pre-Socratic philosopher Heraclitus articulated many ideas that existed in the oral culture that preceded him, but which that culture had been unable to fully articulate and clarify. In some of his most mysterious fragments, each of which deal with the nature of life and death, we can find the solution to this paradox.

First I will offer one of my favorite Heraclitus fragments. It represents an exceptionally tight and compact construction that can only be translated with inelegance and difficulty. The Greek reads:

> *Athanatoi thnetoi, thnetoi athanatoi, zontese ton ekeinon thanaton, ton de ekeinon bion tethneotes.*[45]

I've translated the fragment myself, imperfectly to be sure, in order to capture its tense pithy nature. Standard translations tend to clarify through increased wordiness:

> Immortal mortals, mortal immortals—one living the death of the other, the other dying the former's life.

---

44 Things can get pretty complicated with etymology, and the Latin *anima* is derived from the Greek *anemos*, meaning wind, even though later *anima* is understood to be the Latin equivalent for *psyche*.

45 Heraclitus, fragment 62.

Before hazarding an interpretation, I will add several other fragments in order to build up an appropriate series of echoes and resonances of key ideas that will be central to our interpretation. First the equally mysterious fragment 26:

> A person in the night kindles a light for himself, since his vision has been extinguished. In his sleep he touches that which is dead, when awake he touches that which sleeps.[46]

And here are the fragments that tie these mysterious statements about death, life, and sleep into the elements and our earlier theme of breath, wind, and air:

> Fire lives the death of earth and air lives the death of fire, water lives the death of air, earth that of water.[47]

> Fire's death is birth for air, and air's death birth for water.[48]

> The same thing is the living and dead and the waking and sleeping and young and old. For one changed around is the other and the other changed around is the one.[49]

What these fragments present is a series of transformations, each of which is understood in terms of sleep, life, and death. What is death for one thing, for example earth, is life for another, in this case fire. Fire therefore "lives the death" of earth. It is a similar sense in which the gods "die the life" of mortals and mortals "live the death" of gods, making gods and people "immortal mortals and mortal immortals."

This permeability between divinity and humanity needs to be stressed and remembered. It is no wild innovation on the part of Heraclitus, but rather well attested to in Greek and numerous other pagan myths: heroes can be made into gods. One such example occurs when the immortal sea nymph Calypso offers Odysseus ambrosia (the food of the gods) which would make him immortal if he ate it. Something similar could be said of Ganymede, who is made into a divinity through the will of Zeus. The wall between mortals and immortals is permeable, with entities on either side having the chance to move to the other. In fact, any talk of a wall is mistaken, for what we are really dealing with here is a spectrum. Plants, animals, humans, part-divine

---

46 Heraclitus, T.M. Robinson translation with minor alterations.
47 Heraclitus, fragment 76a.
48 Heraclitus, fragment 76b.
49 Heraclitus, fragment 88. Translation is my own, tortured as it is.

heroes, monsters, nymphs, gods: all rest on a spectrum in terms of what life and death means for them.

This same spectrum is captured in the movement from one element to another. Thus, the movement from living body to corpse consists in the loss of an element of fire and air in the earthly and watery body. The air, as *psyche*, escapes when the fire of the warmth of the body dies and turns into the cold water of the decaying corpse.[50]

The precise mechanics of this process are unimportant; what is crucial here is the recognition that, within an all-living cosmos, death appears as a variation on life and is a type of life. Death is, in fact, a comparative and relative term, rather than an absolute one. This is not the case in most monotheistic metaphysics, in which something is immutable and eternal (such as the soul). The Homeric *psyche* is far from being the full personality of the person who died, nor is it eternal. In most cases it is an empty shade without awareness or self-control. It can be made aware through human interaction, for example through being offered sacrifices and blood, and some special dead maintain full personality, but this is far from the rule.

This theme of the well-being of the dead depending on the attentions and actions of the living is particularly important when we consider practices of ancestor veneration more generally. These practices prove surprisingly durable throughout millennia of monotheistic dominance, even when the dependence of the dead upon the living becomes obscured. In this regard, *psyche* can degrade or evolve as well as having, within some traditions, the chance to find new watery and earthly bodies. *Psyche* remains, throughout its existence, both a principle of change and an object of ongoing change.

There is one final Heraclitus fragment I've offered that still needs to be considered. It states that when we sleep we touch what is dead and, when awake, we touch what sleeps. This again is part of this concept of a spectrum, but now this spectrum is one of awareness that runs from waking, to sleeping, to death, and each point on the spectrum touches the one below it. There is an immediate obviousness here: there is something of death in the loss of control, activity, and awareness that occurs in sleep. We have moved down the spectrum when we sleep, a step closer to death. But there is also a metaphysical and theological aspect to this: sleep is understood to bridge

---

50 Ultimately the elemental theory Heraclitus is working with will be inadequate to capture the full high pagan view, but it does provide us with some valuable insights that will be useful in working back towards this view. It should be kept in mind that the reduction to abstract basic elements is foreign to high pagan oral thought. It is an innovation only made thinkable through writing.

the world of the living and the Underworld.

This idea of sleep touching death is also well attested to in the ancient world, and it is not original to Heraclitus. It was (and still is in many cultures) a common truth that the dead speak to us in our sleep. More potently, there is a longstanding tradition in both Greek and Roman culture that dreams come through two gates, a gate of truth and one of falsehood, and both gates are found in the Underworld land of the dead. In fact, sleep and dream are often identified with the gates to the Underworld. Thus, in the *Odyssey*, Penelope presents the idea of the two gates of dream, and later Virgil clarifies the myth in the *Aeneid* and makes clear that these gates of dream are the entrance and exit from the Underworld itself:

> Two gates for ghostly dreams there are: one gateway
> of honest horn, and one of ivory.
> Issuing by the ivory gate are dreams
> of glimmering illusion, fantasies,
> but those that come through solid polished horn
> may be borne out, if mortals only know them.[51]

> There are two gates of Sleep, one said to be
> Of horn, whereby the true shades pass with ease,
> The other all white ivory agleam
> Without a flaw, and yet false dreams are sent
> Through this one by the ghosts to the upper world.[52]

The first passage is Homer and the second is Virgil. In Virgil's story, Aeneas has journeyed to the Underworld and then must return to the world above through one of the gates of sleep and dream. Sleep is closely tied to death in literary and mythological tradition from the time of high Greek paganism to that of late Roman paganism. Further, sleep is also a precursor to the change in state that occurs more completely in death, making clear once more the highly permeable nature of any boundaries in the pagan world. Even as humans could become gods, and gods could become mortal, so too could life and death pass between each other and mingle along many points of the spectrum.

---

51 Homer, Robert Fitzgerald, and Seamus Heaney, *The Odyssey* (London: David Campbell Publishers, 2000), XIX 652–57.

52 Virgil, Robert Fitzgerald, and Philip R. Hardie, *The Aeneid* (London: David Campbell Publishers, 2000), VI 1211–15.

The fragment that claims we touch sleep while awake and touch death while sleeping begins in a rather odd way. It starts: "A person in the night kindles a light for himself, since his vision has been extinguished," before continuing with its reflections concerning sleep and death. There are linguistic oddities here which are necessary for understanding it; they are also exceptionally challenging to interpret. The word translated here as "kindles" and then later as "touches" ("touches that which is dead... touches that which sleeps") is the same word, *haptetai*. This word can mean both "touches" and "kindles" and, while it is usually a wise strategy to translate the same word in the same way within a given passage, few translators have been able to make this work.

This passage could also mean that a man "touches a candle in the night" or that we "kindle that which is dead" when asleep. In fact, it is fair to assume that Heraclitus meant both of these meanings, which suggests that in the darkness of sleep we kindle a connection to the dead in order to achieve "light" in our sleep. Also, our stumbling into death while sleeping is analogous to burning yourself with a candle at night, because we are made clumsy by the darkness. That is, death is enlightening while we sleep and also endangering and painful. Similarly, our connection to sleep or dream could be understood to be both enlightening and endangering while we are awake.

We can also add to this the potential reading that "kindling" the dead and "kindling sleep" indicates that the lower levels of the spectrum receive fire and life from our living or sleeping being; they take energy through our contact. Our connection with the dead in sleep feeds them, strengthens them through a sharing of fire and energy, just as our waking day provides us with the energy we use while adventuring in dream.

Fragment 26 sets up a tight resonance between vision and awareness.[53] The first sentence deals with the vision differences between day and night, while the second deals with the difference in awareness between waking, sleeping, and death. However, this difference in terms of vision is given a thoroughly *bodily* basis. If we take seriously the relation of fire to air to water and so on, we see more in the flame of the candle than just a source of light. The candle adds fire to the darkness, as the presence of the sleeper adds fire to the watery realm of the dead. Our warmth, our fire, literally kindles the dead to life while we meet them in sleep.[54]

---

53   As a reminder: "A person in the night kindles a light for himself, since his vision has been extinguished. In his sleep he touches that which is dead, when awake he touches that which sleeps."

54   This is important because it casts a reading that may, to our minds influenced heavily by modern philosophy, appear to be about consciousness into a far less mentalistic and abstract form in terms of an

Bodies and Gods

One way to understand this spectrum of lives and deaths is in terms of the body and the distinctions between different types of bodies. This was the point of my earlier description of *psyche* as a body within the body. The *psyche* is an aerial body, the breath of life, within our more familiar body. Neither is to be given absolute priority, as each contributes something to the temporary whole (that is our current life) that neither can accomplish alone.

To think of the spectrum of types of life in terms of body is to recognize that what we consider life or death at any given stage of this process is, in fact, a change within bodies or transformations of one type of body into another. We still recognize this no matter how much our metaphysics attempts to push against it. While we call a corpse "dead," on further reflection is it clear that this is quite false. Many of the cells of the body still live, and as it decomposes it becomes in some ways even more alive with various types of life than it was before it "died." No body is ever dead. Rather, a human corpse is only dead in regard to a *certain* type of life represented by a *certain* type of body.

The difference between our standard bodies and the *psyche* will again be a difference between different types of bodies, one denser and one finer for example. The same will be true for the difference between mortal and immortal bodies, as well as a vast array of differences within the types of bodies of the gods.

Within a high pagan culture, the gods have bodies and the gods are bodies. Without body, it is unclear to an oral pagan culture what it would mean for something to exist.[55] In high pagan myth, the gods have bodies, they eat and drink, they are born, they have sex, and they give birth. They can also be injured. The Greeks had unique words for the special food the gods eat (*ambrosia*) and drink (*nectar*), the Hindu myths have similar concepts (*amrita*).[56] There was also a word for the special blood the gods bleed (ichor) that was closely related to the concept of both ambrosia and nectar.

The types of bodies of the gods do not allow for any simple taxonomy. In fact, one of the main characteristics of many (but not all) divine bodies is their

---

exchange of bodily properties. Our vision, at night, is literally "extinguished." It has lost its fire and the candle flame provides it back, as the fire has departed from the dead who can be "kindled" by sharing in our own flame.

55 I'll discuss in a moment some concepts we should not equate this point with, such as the idea of materialism, so keep this point in mind.

56 *Ambrosia* and *amrita* are linguistically connected, and all three terms (*ambrosia*, *nectar*, *amrita*) translate roughly to "immortality" or "undying."

ability to change from one form to another in almost every imaginable varia-tion. Zeus, for example, doesn't just become animals of various sorts, but can even become a lightning bolt or a golden rain. The changeability of the gods is such a basic part of their nature that it becomes one of the main aspects of high paganism that Plato dedicated himself to attacking.[57]

The bodies of the gods are not at all foreign to our own experience. The earth itself is a goddess, and not in some symbolic or spiritual sense. The earth on which we walk, that gives birth to the plants around us, is the fertile body of Gaia according to Hesiod. Her children, amongst the better-known divinities like Kronos and Rheia, include mountains, hills, and rivers, each of which are themselves understood as living divine bodies. It is not that rivers have gods, but rather that rivers themselves are gods.

Nowhere is this clearer than in the very literal and dramatic battle between Achilles and the river Scamander in Book Twenty-One of the *Iliad*:

And now the deep-whirling river called aloud to Apollo:
"Shame, lord of the silver bow, Zeus' son; you have not kept
the counsels of Kronion, who very strongly ordered you
to stand by the Trojans and defend them, until the sun setting
at last goes down and darkens all the generous ploughland."
He spoke: and spear-famed Achilleus leapt into the middle water
with a spring from the bluff, but the river in a boiling surge was
     upon him
and rose making turbulent all his waters, and pushed off
the many dead men whom Achilleus had killed piled in abundance
in the stream; these, bellowing like a bull, he shoved out
on the dry land, but saved the living in the sweet waters
hiding them under the huge depths of the whirling current.
And about Achilleus in his confusion a dangerous wave rose
up, and beat against his shield and pushed it. He could not
brace himself with his feet...
so always the crest of the river was overtaking Achilleus
for all his speed of foot, since gods are stronger than mortals.

---

57   These attacks relied upon the idea that a (abstractly) perfect entity can't possibly change.

And every time swift-footed brilliant Achilleus would begin
to turn and stand and fight the river, and try to discover
if all the gods who hold the wide heaven were after him, every
time again the enormous wave of the sky-fed river
would strike his shoulders from above.[58]

For the Ancient Greeks, there are gods *of* rivers and there are gods that *are* rivers. There are both gods of the sea such as Poseidon, and the god that *is* the ocean, Oceanus. There is the goddess of the earth, Demeter, and also the goddess earth Gaia. There is the god of the sky, Zeus, and the god that *is* heaven, Ouranos. The bodies of these gods are the world, and put together they are the cosmos. To tie this to our earlier discussion, nature or *phusis* is alive because it consists first and primarily of the bodies of undying gods and then, later, in the more mortal bodies of plants and animals.

The Primacy of Bodies in Pagan Metaphysics

Pagan animism understands everything that exists in terms of living bodies. The more common distinctions between living and dead are actually distinctions between types of bodies and the changes that occur to bodies, such that nothing is ever "dead" in an absolute sense but only dead to a certain type of life.

This conception of the body is the origin of the idea that the "sum is greater than the whole of its parts." A body is not an arrangement constituted out of parts, but rather is a whole that alone constitutes the parts of which it is made. A hand cannot be a hand without a body; it is not possible to put together a collection of various body parts pre-existing the body to create a total body. The same goes for the body that is the earth, and the many other bodies that make up the cosmos. One can't have a mountain without a valley, and without a range or plain. One can't have a river without the land through which it passes, or a tree without the earth it grips and sky it upholds.

This nature of the body overlaps and provides content to the associative nature of oral thought we have already discussed. In an associative logic, something is understood in terms of the multiplicity of relations that constitute their reality. These relations, however, are not constituent *parts* but rather larger patterns and webs; only in these patterns does a thing take on its meaning.

---

58 Homer and Lattimore, *Iliad* Book XXI (Chicago: Univ. of Chicago Press, 2011), 229–42, 263–69.

The associative ontology that corresponds to the associative logic of oral cultures is the ontology of bodies.

Bodies are incompatible with reductionist approaches. A body can't be built up, but rather must be understood holistically from the whole down. This is the reason that our earlier discussion of the elements of earth, air, fire, and water is ultimately more deceptive than informative. It was useful in helping us to see in what sense the *psyche* might be a body within a body, but beyond that it is a rather dangerous model not truly fit to oral high pagan cultures.

Thinking in terms of base elements is a standard form, in fact the earliest form, of materialism. Thus, our focus on this in Heraclitus risks shifting our focus from high paganism to a period when writing had already allowed for the conception of an abstract materialism. We see this materialism in many of the Pre-Socratic philosophers who produced work around the time of Heraclitus, particularly in Anaximenes who "attributed all the causes of things to infinite air, and did not deny that there were gods, or pass them over in silence; yet he believed not that air was made by them, but that they arose from air."[59]

This view reaches a pinnacle in Empedocles, who proposed that the entire cosmos is constituted by the four elements, and the forces of love and hate cause the various combinations that make everything that is. Such reductive materialisms do away with any robust understanding of body, and in fact can't distinguish between a random pile of stuff and a unified body. They are very far from the metaphysics of high pagan culture.

Body takes priority, then, over any reductive explanation or description of its constituent parts, but not over its relations. Bodies are always interpenetrating and interpenetrated, always defined by what they do and the way they are acted upon as well as by their interior self-organizing impetus.

Bodies and *Psyche*

There are two very common modes of thought applied to bodies in monotheistic metaphysics, neither of which capture the high pagan view of bodies. The first is the reductive materialism found in much contemporary science and the thought of Anaximenes and Empedocles we have already discussed. The second is that favored by both Plato and Aristotle, which is to propose an abstract and often spiritual non-material organizing principle that makes a body a body.

---

59 Augustine discussing Anaximenes. Augustine, *The City of God Against the Pagans* VIII (Cambridge: Cambridge University Press, 1998), 2.

In both Plato and Aristotle, such a principle is called a Form (or *eidos*), though each means rather different things by this term. Despite that difference, in both we see an abstract principle of order and organization. For Plato and the Neo-Platonists this principle is non-material and transcendental and plays both a totalizing and reductive role. For Aristotle, this principle is embodied in matter and eventually becomes seen as the Soul, especially by the heavily Aristotelian church philosophy of the medieval period.

In Archaic Greece, however, the *psyche* will not be the ultimate organizing principle of the body, though it will be what provides the self-moving impetus to the body. As already presented, *psyche* and the more standard body are engaged in a complex partnership, rather than a division between chaotic matter and order. As I have stated, *psyche* should best be understood as a body within the body, each body having its own particular powers and properties and neither complete without the other.

Because bodies are understood as holistic, organized entities rather than something constituted by particular types of matter or elements, they can't be understood in terms of the standard materialistic approaches common to our times. For example, the fact that the *psyche* is a body within a body does not mean that we can, as some fringe researchers have attempted to do, weigh the "soul" to prove that there is a substantial material soul that leaves the body at death. Similarly, evidence of a presence of a body is not necessarily tied to the presence of a specific type of material or energy signature. In fact, any such correlation will depend entirely upon what type of body we are discussing.

Take for example the following argument: *Waves in the ocean do not exist because I measured all the material in a given location where a wave was supposed to be and found only water, just like in the rest of the ocean. Therefore, there is no material proof of the existence of waves.* This argument clearly looks for the wrong type of thing and misunderstands the type of body that a wave is.

At this point it can be useful to think, instead, of body in terms of pattern. A normal human body will be a pattern in a given material, but other bodies will be made out of different materials and perhaps many materials.

To put the point directly and provocatively, the body of some spirit may be present in a séance room as the organized patterns that arise in the motions of the things that make up the room. It can also be present as the experiences and thoughts of those within the room. You need not find something else, other than the ordinary constituents of the room, because it is in the pattern and relations amongst those objects: in fact, it is in the *meanings* arising out of these relations where the body of the spirit is. To insist upon extra matter or non-standard energy fluctuations of a given sort is to miss the point. Some bodies will be accompanied by these, like a bubble in the ocean, but others will not, such as waves or currents.

We have now drawn our high pagan animism into conversation with contemporary approaches dominated by monotheistic thinking, which would either totalize things from above (via abstract organizing principles) or reduce things to basic constituents (via reductive materialism). The ubiquity of abstraction, reduction, and totalization within our monotheistic thought patterns also infects many contemporary concepts of animism. One of the most common "infections" found in contemporary animism is the urge to understand what it means to say *all things are living* in terms of *all things having "minds" or "spirit."* For ancient animisms, however, there are no firm distinctions between minds, spirits, and bodies. As I stressed, the word that sometimes means mind, soul, or spirit in Greek can be and should be (at least in the Archaic context) understood as a type of body. All bodies live; thus, saying they live does not also mean that all bodies have minds or spirits, unless we are talking about very specific types of body combinations such as our own. In fact, to focus on the mind and/or the soul as the foundation of life or human existence is to engage in a specific type of reduction: the body becomes merely a suit of clothes, or a prison, or an object that the soul drives around.

In other words, pagan animism rejects the dualisms of mind vs. body and soul vs. body, while many contemporary forms of animism make these dualisms absolute. Here we must notice the lesson we learn from understanding death as relative and actually just a distinction between different types of life. Dualistic animism would leave open the door to imagining what the cosmos would be if its "spirit" departed: consider the concept of the "universal soul" that plays such a major role in versions of Neoplatonism and Gnosticism. For Homer, the cosmos could never be a dead, as in absolutely dead, body.

This type of mistake is what happens in most common forms of panpsychism. Usually panpsychism means that everything has "psyche" in the contemporary sense (that is, mind). But if we take it literally, in the original sense, it would mean that all things have *psyche* in the ancient sense; in other words, all things have the breath of life. This would also be a mistake, as clearly the breath part of life is rather unique to only certain types of life. There is no doctrine that survives, nor would there likely have been at the time, but I hazard to say that living rivers probably don't have *psyche*, nor do many other gods and plants. Later, Aristotle will attempt to break down different parts, aspects, or types of soul that capture these differences. His thinking in terms of reductive soul and soul-types is not true to the pagan view, but his overall recognition that there are different types of lives and ways of living (in other words, different types of body) does capture the high pagan view.

From Consciousness to Action

Contemporary animisms and panpsychism attempt to understand the "life" all things are presumed to share in terms of consciousness. Consciousness, and especially the focus and obsession with it, is a major artifact of a specific turn that occurred in modern philosophy. That turn was itself a further development of the obsession with the non-material found in Plato. The view we are presenting instead is one that existed before the artificial dualism of matter and mind/spirit/soul/consciousness.

Oral societies don't think about "consciousness" the way that we do. For them, being-aware is something we and our bodies do, not something that we have or are. The action of *paying attention* only gets turned into an abstract entity or property with the rise of writing, which pushes us to turn verbs and action words into timeless nouns. To say that everything is alive can mean that everything has agency, but not necessarily that everything has consciousness. Indeed, there is more confusion involved in the statement that we "have consciousness" than there is truth or illumination.

Having agency, however, does mean that everything is capable of response or of some sort of communication if the thing is so inclined. Consciousness is not necessary in order to learn, for example, as much of what I do on a daily basis and much of what I communicate occurs without overtly self-aware or conscious thought. We act, speak, think and only in moments of breakdown do we reflect in such a way as to "become conscious" of these things. To capture the high pagan view of the cosmos, we must resist the urge to turn the action of "focusing on something" into "having awareness." We must also resist the ultimate point this mistake pushes toward: "being awareness." Anytime contemporary animism or panpsychism turns to talk of consciousness, we have fallen into anthropomorphism. We have also assumed what is obviously false: that to have life *must* mean to have a life like ours in terms of some particularly privileged element. If anything, the pagan gods and plethora of divine and semi-divine entities should make clear that most life is very much not like ours.

I will conclude this chapter by providing an answer to a colleague that has been a long time coming, which ties into the subject we are discussing. On one of my essays on *Gods and Radicals* arguing against transcendent conceptions of the gods and the Otherworld, the exceptionally insightful Christopher Scott Thompson asked how I account for seemingly transcendental mystical experiences.[60] In other words, the this-worldly anti-transcendental focus on bodies I have provided in this chapter seems undermined by the possibility of having mystical experiences in which one overcomes one's own individuality, bodily limits, and type of life. Doesn't this show that we are more than our bodies and the type of life we currently experience? Doesn't it also show that there is something other than this world that exists transcendent of time and space?

I have been practicing various forms of meditation and mysticism for over twenty years and have had many experiences that lend themselves to the description "transcendental," experiences that seem to involve transcendence of both time and space, as well as personal identity or ego. There are undoubtedly experiences that escape our ability to describe or understand in terms of our normal concepts and language. Here, the permeability of types of life and bodies comes into play, the fuzzy nature of any firm boundaries we would seek to draw around anything in the cosmos. If our everyday concepts of life and death mark differences in types of life and bodies and differing points on a spectrum (or in a field of possible lives and bodies), then the experience of sleep and dream as we have already discussed is a model for mystical experience. As mortals can become immortal, so too can they experience temporarily what it is like to be a divinity, as we also come to experience the dead through our interrelated "kindling" or "touching" in sleep, in trance, in meditation.

Spectrums can imply hierarchies or extremes, neither of which apply to these transformations of bodies. So, our talk of a spectrum should give way to that of a field. Mystical experience can be understood as a temporary and partial bodily transformation from one mode of life to another, and the potentially available bodies and lives which we can experience are hypothetically beyond limit. This accounts for the profound bodily and worldly changes,

---

60 Author of *Pagan Anarchism*, which I highly recommend to you.

benefits, and risks involved in mystical experience and practice. Ultimately, it is not just the lives of gods or the dead we can temporarily embody, but also those of animals, plants, daimons, temporal or spatial locations, even something like sky itself, and so on. All that lives can, at least hypothetically and perhaps only temporarily and partially, be lived by another, should the proper method be found. And in the pagan cosmos everything lives.

THIRD INTERLUDE
The Greek Magical Papyri

The most majestic goddess' child was set
Aflame as an initiate—and on
The highest mountain peak was set aflame—
And fire did greedily gulp seven springs
Of wolves, seven of bears, seven of lions,
But seven dark-eyed maidens with dark urns
Drew water and becalmed the restless fire.[61]

Adonai... These are the words: Accomplish all that I have written on this
for you, and I will leave the east and the west where he was established
formerly, and I will preserve the flesh of Osiris always and I will not
break the bonds with which you bound Typhon, and I will not call those
who have died a violent death but will leave them alone, and I will not
pour out the oil of Syrian cedar but will leave it alone, and I will save
Ammon and not kill him, and I will not scatter the limbs of Osiris, and
I will hide you from the giants... Isis, holy maiden, give me a sign of the
things that are going to happen, reveal your holy veil, shake your black
Tyche and move the constellation of the bear.[62]

O master Oserapis and the gods who sit with Oserapis, I pray to you, I
Artemisie, daughter of Amasi.[63]

---

61 All excerpts from the *Greek Magical Papyri* are from Hans Dieter Betz, *The Greek Magical Papyri* (Chica-
    go: Chicago Univ. Press, 1986). PGM XX 4–12 with minor alterations. Second–first century BC.
62 PGM LVII 1–37 with minor alterations, first century AD.
63 PGM XL 1–18, fourth century AD.

It is common in our day and age to think of religion in terms of dogmatism, commitment, faith, and absolutism. In other words, we are accustomed to members of one religion assuming, almost by default, that all other religions are wrong. It can be hard to appreciate that these aspects were rather foreign to pagan culture generally. Pagan cultures are usually marked by a deep religious curiosity, even a gluttonous hunger for new practices, new gods, new rituals, and new wisdom. The Athenians enjoyed celebrating new mystery cults and religious ceremonies whenever they heard of them, and the Romans frequently imported the gods and religious practices of the peoples they conquered. In each case the new traditions were practiced alongside the pre-existing religious practices of the culture, without general conflict or concern. Indeed, one of the oldest gods of the Greeks, Dionysus, was nonetheless understood as a foreign god who migrated to Greece. This understanding existed despite the fact that he was historically anything but foreign; instead, he was a god of Otherness, of openness to the foreign and new. As such, Dionysus held a central role in Greek history longer than many of the other gods believed by the Greeks to be local.

Kwasi Wiredu discusses a similar attitude in the Akan people of Ghana, Africa, one that he identifies with an empirical approach to questions of religion. The Akan, Wiredu points out, would frequently try out new gods and determine their attitude towards them based on how efficacious their rites proved to be. Similarly, old gods could be abandoned and even "killed" through being ignored and their shrines neglected if they proved to no longer work as people desired.

A similar attitude on the part of the Igbo people of Nigeria towards foreign gods and practices is captured in Chinua Achebe's historically based novel, *Things Fall Apart*. In that meticulously researched work, Achebe makes clear the difference in approach of the Igbo people and the Christian missionaries who take over their culture. For the Igbo, the new ideas of the Christians are strange and often ridiculous, but they feel no need to dogmatically claim they are wrong. In fact, they offer instead to include the new gods of the Christians within their own community and see how things work out. The Christians, on the other hand, repeatedly insist that the Igbo do not understand what they are saying and that the Igbo gods simply do not exist.

It is a sad fact that part of what facilitated the European and American rape of Africa was the open, curious, and pluralistic attitude of many traditional African cultures. This same sad story is found frequently enough in the relations between Native American cultures and the European invaders. The First Nations exhibited an open curiosity and friendly exchange of ideas, in comparison with the absolutist insistence on the fundamental wrongness of the native views.

To be sure, the official state religions of pagan cultures such as those enshrined by Athenian, Spartan, or Roman governments often sought to enforce various forms of orthodoxy for the sake of political domination. When it served their purposes, the political forces were willing to kill those they might accuse of impiety, as occurred with Socrates. But these were clearly cynical moves, in contrast with the overall nature of the cultures within which such things occurred, as epitomized by the popular religion rather than the state sanctioned cults and practices.[64] The key point is that the transition between high and late pagan cultures happened piece-meal and extended over centuries of time, just as the transition from oral to literate society took several centuries to solidify. Each transition occurred first at the level of the state and the privileged circles of society, while the people more generally maintained the old insights and practices for longer periods of time. This is largely the origin of the term "pagan" to begin with: in Italy, the cities were faster to convert to Christianity, while the rural countryside held to the old ways for much longer.

Although dating from the late pagan period, the *Greek Magical Papyri* provide us with an interesting insight into the survival of the fundamentally high pagan popular culture through the Hellenistic period begun by Alexander the Great's conquests, through the dominance of the Roman Republic and Empire, and into the early Christian era.

At the start of this interlude I offered three pieces from the Greek Magical Papyri spanning five centuries, from the second or first century BC for the first selection, the first century AD for the second, and the fourth century AD for the third. The first is a spell identified with a woman from Syria, "The Charm of the Syrian Woman of Gadara."[65] Other than this fact, there are few cultural or religious markers in the charm—most of the oldest pieces in the papyri are rather brief. The second selection contains the gods of three different religions all used together, specifically Adonai of Hebrew origin; Osiris, Isis, and Ammon of the Egyptians; and Typhon and Tyche of the

---

64 For an extensive discussion of the tensions between popular religion and state religion in the pagan Mediterranean see the excellent discussion offered by Jake Stratton-Kent in his *Geosophia*.
65 Ancient Gadara was a city in what is now Jordan.

Greeks. The third fragment deals with Oserapis or Serapis, an Egyptian god formed specifically to appeal to Greeks and largely adopted throughout the Greek-speaking world of the Hellenistic period, which included Egypt.

The papyri represent a massive collection of magical rituals, spells, charms, remedies, and guidelines for the practitioner aimed at all manner of goals and purposes. In fact, as argued persuasively by Jake Stratton-Kent, they are the missing link between ancient pagan magico-religious practices and modern grimoire magic (such as those represented by the various so-called "Keys of Solomon"). These papyri are where the now rather famous "Headless" or "Bornless" ritual was found.[66] This massive collection as we have it now is likely the outcome of a collector gathering together smaller, but equally diverse, collections used by professional magicians in the Hellenistic and Roman world. In other words, these papyri represent "magician's notebooks," much in the style of modern versions such as *The Grimoire of Author Gauntlet* or the impressive collection of notes and operations capture in the recently named and published *Book of Oberon*.

It seems magicians have always been mad collectors—and indeed utilizers—of rituals, spells, and insights from many religious and cultural contexts. In this, despite what gods they might appeal to, their concrete practice and overall collector's spirit resemble paganism more than anything else. The papyri, then, represent the working notes of practicing magicians, many of them passed down from one to the next. These magicians also mostly acted outside the authority and oversight of official state religious apparatuses.

The eclecticism and syncretism displayed in the papyri, also found in the practices of magicians and cunning folk of all kinds throughout history, has sometimes been described as a new religion arising from the multicultural environment of the conquests and empires of Alexander and Rome. Others have more perceptively pointed out that the pre-classical Archaic Mediterranean world (which I have been including within the category of high paganism) was itself a wildly interconnected one where religious and occult mixing was the rule, rather than the exception. That is, the rule of the pagan world had always been eclecticism and syncretism: what is displayed in the

---

66 The "Bornless" or "Headless" ritual was one of the earliest pieces of the *Greek Magical Papyri* to make it into modern occult thinking through its influence on the Golden Dawn and later by its extensive use by Aleister Crowley. Crowley used it to contact his Holy Guardian Angel. Since then it is has a very popular ritual for a variety of purposes within ceremonial magic. Crowley's recreation of the ritual can be found in his *Liber Samekh* For examples of more recent reflections on the ritual see Jake Stratton-Kent's *The Headless One* and Chapter Three of Gordon White's *The Chaos Protocols*.

papyri is better understood as both a survival and re-invigoration of the cultural milieu that would have been found in the Archaic oral period. Thus, A.A. Barb argues that "much that we are accustomed to see classified as late 'syncretism' is rather the ancient and original, deep-seated popular religion, coming to the surface when the whitewashing of 'classical' writers and artists begins to peel off."[67]

The papyri do indeed represent a wild and often disorienting collection. In them we find spells using the authority of Greek, Egyptian, Babylonian, Hebrew, Canaanite, and Christian gods. Even in the Greek contexts we have mixes of generally popular gods and less common Orphic and Neoplatonic manifestations of the gods. We find Zeus, Dionysus, Tyche, Kronos and Chronos, Typhon and Hekate, Demeter and Artemis, Aion and Helios, amongst many other Greek gods.[68] Amongst Hebrew and Canaanite influences we find Adonai, Sabaoth, Iao, Michael, and Gabriel. We find Christian references to Christos and the Holy Trinity of Father, Son, and Holy Spirit. We find the Persian and Roman Mithras. We find the Babylonian Ereschigal, identified frequently with the Greek Hekate. We find the Egyptian Hathor, Thoth, Harpocrates, and many more.

These goddesses and gods do not at all appear in appropriate orthodox isolation in separate hymns or spells. Neither are they consistently placed in hierarchical relationships, though identifying divinities from different cultural origins with one another is not uncommon in the texts. But in one and the same spell one might find, as in our second example, a prayer to the Hebrew Adonai containing references to the Greek Typhon and Tyche and Egyptian Osiris and Ammon, and then concluding with a prayer to Isis. In terms of religious loyalties, the *Greek Magical Papyri* are not Jewish, Christian, Egyptian, Persian, Babylonian, or Greek. Similarly, though there are strong Neoplatonic and Orphic influences, and we can see the clear development of what will become later Gnosticism in the text, the general Neoplatonic metaphysics and theology (which I would claim is monotheistic) is largely lacking from the papyri.

There can be no question that a majority of the papyri are clearly what we would call chthonic. Throughout most of the texts there is a strong presence,

---

67 A.A. Barb, "Three Elusive Amulets," JWCI 27 (1964).

68 The history of the god Chronos/Kronos is a complicated and fascinating one, largely consisting of the original king of the Titans and father of Zeus being distinguished, in Orphic and Neoplatonic thought, from the god of time who was identified with a nearly identical name to only later then have this earlier artificial distinction collapsed back into one entity.

power, and threat from the dead; solar gods such as Helios show up in their older original worldly forms, rather than representing any type of transcendence. Indeed, the papyri are almost devoid of concepts of transcendence and instead focus on worldly powers and divinities, even if gods we are more used to finding in transcendental contexts are drawn upon.[69] Thus, as their editor puts it, in the papyri "the underworld deities, the demons and spirits of the dead, are constantly and unscrupulously invoked and exploited as the most important means for achieving the goals of human life on earth: the acquisition of love, wealth, health, fame, knowledge of the future, control over other persons, and so forth. In other words, there is a consensus that the best way to success and worldly pleasures is by using the underworld, death, and the forces of death."[70] The key thing to realize is that the anti-transcendental and Archaic nature of this focus on the dead present and contiguous with the living goes along with the recognition of the worldly and bodily nature of the gods.

To get a better sense of the flavor of the mixing that occurs in the papyri, allow me to share a few of the charms that are particularly interesting. One, called a "Charm to Hekate Ereschigal against fear of punishment" actually contains several different charms, some to protect against various threatening spirits and others to influence the love of others. One of these charms of protection reads: "I am Ereschigal, the one holding her thumbs, and not even one evil can befall her." A second, stronger one, includes the symbolic proof of the practitioner's initiation into the secrets of the underworld: "I have been initiated, and went down into the underground chamber of the Dactyles, and I saw the other things down below, Ereschigal, virgin, bitch, serpent, wreath, key, herald's wand, golden sandal of the lady of Tartaros."[71] This particular charm is to be said at the crossroads where, it clarifies, Hekate Ereschigal comes.

The various cultural markers present in the charms must be stressed. We find those of the Babylonian Ereschigal, a goddess of the Underworld, and the myth of her sister Inanna's journey to the Underworld (which the strange list of objects and symbols indirectly references). We find as well

---

69 Hans Dieter Betz, in his introduction to the papyri, claims that "gods like Hermes, Aphrodite and even the Jewish god Iao, have in many respects become underworld deities" in the papyri. He misses the fact that each of these divinities had an older and original chthonic and underworld aspect that the papyri draw on.

70 Betz, "Introduction" to *The Greek Magical Papyri*, xlvii.

71 PGM LXX 6-11.

the Greek Hekate, along with the reference to Tartaros, the darkest part of the Greek Underworld. Finally, we have the Greek legendary Dactyles, who were frequently identified with the male guardians of the Titan goddess Rhea, amongst many other ancient traditions.[72] The series of charms ends with the creation of a cake used to steal the sleep of a victim through the use of the name Hekate.[73]

I must confess to the fourth papyri of the *Greek Magical Papyri* being my favorite. It is one of the largest of the papyri, and dates from the fourth century AD. The reason I love it is that it contains several absolutely beautiful and, at times terrifying, invocations to the moon at different stages of its cycle. The moon is variously identified with different goddesses but largely the name of Hekate dominates amongst them, with the various other goddesses representing phases in Hekate's nature. I'll include parts of three of these hymns, spells, or invocations to conclude these reflections on the *Greek Magical Papyri* and to give you a full sense of the feel of the collection.

Note in these the mixing of various cultural references, especially the obviously Greek; the Egyptian Isis and Osiris; the Hebrew Michael and Adonia; and others. Beyond this, note the wild multiplication of meanings and resonances, many of them in stark contrast, presented in a true paratactic form that captures pluralism without true hierarchy or unity in the style of oral thought and speech:

PGM IV "Document to the waning moon"
Hail, Holy Light, Ruler of Tartaros,
Who strikes with rays; hail, Holy Beam, who whirl
Up out of darkness and subvert all things
With aimless plans...
I now adjure you by this potent night,
In which your light is last to fade away,
In which a dog opens, closes not, its mouth,
In which the bar of Tartaros is opened,
In which forth rages Kerberos, armed with
A thunderbolt, bestir yourself, Mene,
Who need the solar nurse, guard of the dead,
You I implore, Maid, by your stranger beams,
You I implore, O cunning, lofty, swift,

---

72 For an extensive investigation of the role of the Dactyles in the development of Greek magic see Jake Stratton-Kent's *Geosophia*.
73 These charms are all found in PGM LXX 4–25.

O crested one, who draws swords, valiant,
Healer, with forethought, far-famed, goading one,
Swift-footed, brave, crimson, Darkness, Brimo,
Immortal, heedful, Persian, Pastoral,
Alkyone, gold-crowned, the elder goddess,
Shining, sea-goddess, ghostly, beautiful,
The one who shows, skiff-holder, aiming well,
Self-gendered...
You'll, willy-nilly, do this task for me,
Mare, Kore, dragoness, lamp, lightening flash,
Star, lion, she-wolf...
Be wroth, O maid, at him
Foe of heaven's gods, of Helios
Osiris and of Isis, his bedmate.
As I instruct you, hurl him to this ill
Because, Kore, I know your good and great
Majestic names, by which heaven is illumed
And earth drinks dew and is pregnant; from these
The universe increases and declines...
Mistress, Harken-techtha, who sits beside Lord Osiris,
Michael, Archangel of angels, the god who lights the way,
Perform for me.

PGM IV 2520–2565 "The Second Spell"

I offer you this spice, O child of Zeus,
Dart-shooter, Artemis, Persephone,
Shooter of deer, night-shining, triple-sounding,
Triple-voiced, triple headed Selene,
Triple-pointed, triple-faced, triple-necked,
And goddess of the triple ways, who hold
Untiring flaming fire in triple baskets,
And you who oft' frequent the triple way,
And rule the triple decades with three forms
And flames and dogs. From toneless throats you send
A dread, sharp cry when you, O goddess, have
Raised up an awful sound with triple mouths.
Hearing your cry, all worldly things are shaken:
The nether gates and Lethe's holy water
And primal Chaos and the shining chasm
Of Tartaros. At it every immortal

And every mortal man, the starry mountains,
Valleys and every tree and roaring rivers,
And even the restless sea, the lonely echo,
And daimons through the world, shudder at you,
O blessed one, when they hear your dread voice...
Lamp-bearer, shining and aglow, Selene,
Star-coursing, heavenly, torch-bearer, fire-breather,
Woman four-faced, four-named, four-roads' mistress.
Hail, goddess, and attend your epithets,
O heavenly one, harbor goddess, who roam
The mountains and are goddess of the crossroads;
O nether one, goddess of the depths, eternal,
Goddess of dark, come to my sacrifices.

PGM IV. 2708–2784 Spell:

Come, giant Hekate, Dione's guard,
O Persia, Baubo Phroune, dart-shooter,
Unconquered, Lydian, the one untamed,
Sired nobly, torch bearing, guide, who bends down
Proud necks, Kore, hear, you who've parted gates
Of steel unbreakable. O Artemis,
Who, too, were once protectress, mighty-one,
Mistress, who burst forth from the earth, dog-leader,
All-tamer, crossroad goddess, triple-headed,
Bringer of light, august virgin, I call you
Fawn-slayer, crafty, O infernal one,
And many-formed. Come, Hecate, goddess
Of three ways, who with your fire-breathing phantoms
Have been allotted dreaded roads and harsh
Enchantments. Hekate I call you with
Those who untimely passed away and with
Those heroes who have died without a wife
And children, hissing wildly, yearning in
Their hearts...
Gate-breaker; Come Hekate, of fiery
Counsel, I call you to my sacred chants...
Both Orion and Michael who sits on high:
You hold the seven waters
And the earth, keeping in check
The one they call the great serpent...

Io, all power-full goddess,
And Io all-guarding one;
Io, All-sustaining One...
Avenging goddess, strong goddess, rite of ghosts.[74]

This wild multiplication of images, this listing one after another of marks of rank and concrete divine actions, captures both the oral heritage of high Archaic pagan religion (and indeed many of the papyri show clearly the mark of once having been orally composed and passed down) and the pluralistic, embodied, earthly/worldly nature of a true pagan metaphysics. Here we see the outcome of a culture that is open, curious, and generally able to adopt and integrate a wild diversity of different religious, national, and cultural influences without feeling the need for an absolute totalizing hierarchy or reductive metaphysics to dominate the abundance of multiplicity.

The fundamentally pagan nature of much of the papyri becomes all the more important when we consider them in their cultural context. Hekate is one of the most important goddesses in the papyri, and I have sampled from some of the most striking portions that include her, but she was already at the time of the writing of these rituals a central figure in a very different theological tradition.

The papyri that most extensively feature Hekate derive from the third and fourth centuries AD. By then, Hekate was already central to Middle Platonic theology as an abstract goddess personifying the soul of the cosmos, ruling individual souls in their journey to and from the immaterial realm of abstract changeless divinity, as well as mediating semi-divine entities known as daimons. In the second century AD, the *Chaldean Oracles* become a central part of late pagan Platonic thought, a thought that is ultimately monotheist in the centrality of abstract transcendent unity. These texts present Hekate as one of their primary narrators and present a complex Platonic theology and metaphysics.[75] With the dominance of Platonic thinking and the Hekate of the *Chaldean Oracles* in the third and fourth centuries in mind, it becomes clear that the presentation of Hekate in the papyri is part of an active battle with a dominant counter conception

---

74 These quotations from Betz's translation of the papyri are not the full hymns and spells but rather just selections from the larger texts with, at times, minor alterations on my part to improve readability.

75 For an extensive evaluation of the developments which occurred in the ancient understanding of Hekate from her first appearance in the Archaic Greek high pagan period to her centrality in Platonic thought in the *Chaldean Oracles* see Sarah Iles Johnston's *Hekate Soteira*, a work lacking only in its rather brief and inadequate consideration of *The Greek Magical Papyri*.

of her, a pagan war against the increasingly non-pagan Platonic theology of the time.

The papyri, then, stand as proof of the survival of a high pagan perspective and practice in late pagan and early monotheistic periods, practices in contrast with even the state sanctioned religion of late paganism. As such, they provide a nice example for us of what the occult and religious practice of high paganism may have been like. The papyri also demonstrate the unique power of a pagan metaphysics to creatively employ and integrate the multiplicity of human approaches to the divine, without the threat of dogmatism or absolutism.

CHAPTER FOUR
Divine Subjects and Substance:
On Event Ontology

Monotheistic metaphysics was first clearly developed and articulated in the western context by Plato and Aristotle. Each tried to reduce beings to constituent parts, and each attempted to explain change through ultimate totalizing principles and eventually through one unifying principle.[76]

Aristotle claims for change to occur there must be something that changes and something that motivates the change. For Aristotle, these roles will be played by substance and *telos*, or "goal." This is the invention, historically, of what comes to be known as substance ontology, and it has largely dominated our thought in one form or another ever since it was proposed. The main thrust of this chapter is to make clear how the invention of substance ontology is one of the most basic breaks with pagan metaphysics. It is also a lynchpin of the dominance of monotheistic thinking.

The Unmoved Mover

The simple idea of *substance* is that for change to occur there must be something that stays the same throughout the changes. Likewise, there must be a medium for attributes or characteristics to adhere within. All beings must be

---

76 Claims such as this concerning Plato are meant to represent a feasible reading of his work and arguably the most influential reading historically. Personally, I am of the opinion that Plato is much harder to pin down than has generally been the view of most thinkers and scholars, but the points I offer represent the Plato who was enshrined in Neoplatonism and most later thought.

grounded in something, made out of it and ultimately owing their existence to it. This foundation of existence, this stability throughout the course of change, is substance.

To make a thing, however, substance must take on form: it must have some given structure and set of characteristics that are essential to the thing. Thus, we return to our earlier discussion of definition in terms of general category and essential difference. For Aristotle, the substance of mankind is "animal" and our essential form is "reason," thus making us "rational animals." This same dualism can be thought of in terms of form and matter, with matter playing the most common role of substance.[77]

About two millennia later, Descartes will understand the universe in terms of two main types of substance: material substance and thinking substance (which constitutes souls or minds). Whether in Aristotle's terms, or in Descartes', or in terms of subatomic particles, energy, waves in energy fields, multidimensional vibrating strings, or however else we formulate our substance ontology, this point remains the same. Change is derived from the unchanging, and all things are open to some reduction-to-one.

The other side of this picture is the impetus or motivation for change. This brings us to Aristotle's idea of god: the Unmoved Mover, which is the end-goal of all motion and alteration in the universe. All things are ultimately made out of one type of thing, and all things are moving towards one ultimate thing. This idea of god as the source of change takes on numerous forms throughout the history of thought. We are now most familiar with the idea of god as the efficient cause of change: in other words, god creates the universe and provides the energy and being that then leads to all the subsequent changes. God gives the first push to the domino chain that is the universe and the rest follows from it.

For Aristotle, the view is a bit subtler: the Unmoved Mover doesn't give anything a direct push. It doesn't imbue the universe with any particular energy or impetus, but rather provides the goal of perfection that all things aim toward by god's existence itself. By simply existing, the Unmoved Mover motivates things to change, to become more perfect. Here, like almost everywhere else in monotheistic thought, the meaning of perfection will be singular. There will only be one ultimate perfection, and though there are many different types

---

77   Aristotle, at points, claims that matter is substance, form is substance, and form + matter is substance. We will ignore these complications by simply pointing out that substance is the unchanging substrate of what is that provides the ground for change.

of things, each thing is only able to partake in perfection in limited ways. For each thing there will be only one way that they can achieve their type of thing's perfection.

This singular path that each thing has to its highest perfection is understood in terms of that thing's function within the universe, its particular kind of virtue. The virtue of a knife is to cut well and thus be both strong and sharp, the virtue of a human is rational action. The same point can be made in terms of Plato's Form of the Good. The ultimate perfect unchanging Form causes all change through our desire to reach it, each in whatever particular way a thing is able to approach it.

In both Plato and Aristotle's view, whether we think from the ground up or the top down, change always depends on the One. There is no true multiplicity, only the illusion of multiplicity. Put another way, for monotheistic metaphysics, sameness and unity are primitive (that is, foundational and primary), differences are derivative, and are ultimately bad. Plato argues any change that occurs to the perfect can only be a change in the direction of imperfection. Similarly, any difference that enters into existence in contrast to the One will exist as a fall from perfection.

For a pagan metaphysics, on the other hand, change and multiplicity are primary. In fact, it wouldn't be too strong to claim that *Eros* or desire in Hesiod represents the force of change itself as one of the first things to exist, rather than something like a medium, foundation, or goal of change.

Pagan Event Ontology

It is time to draw together several of the points that have already been made in order to present a final key aspect of pagan metaphysics. Chapter One presented a pagan metaphysics as committed to irreducible pluralism. This is a multiplicity without an overriding hierarchy amidst the diversity. Chapter Two presented oral high pagan thought as constituted in terms of an associative relational logic. We saw a focus on active agents and actions over abstract concepts or stable entities. Chapter Three presented this focus on active agents as an understanding of all existing things as living. Here the associative relational logic was understood in terms of an ontology of bodies.

Now we can complete this presentation with one final aspect that ties the previous together: *a pluralistic cosmos of relationally-understood active bodies with agency is best described through an event ontology.* In other words, pagan metaphysics sees actions and events as primitive (primary and foundational). It also rejects the fundamental nature and even the existence of substance, whether that substance is understood as matter (or energy), or spirit (mind, consciousness, soul, etc.), or both.

Although it may not seem obvious, this is the understanding of body I was suggesting previously. When bodies are understood as patterns of activities, patterns within larger patterns (the penetrated and penetrating), body is a way in which various actions and events correspond, associate, and relate. To speak of body is not to speak of matter or substance, but rather to speak of ongoing patterns of change.

To understand this better, we can refer to the early modern philosopher Baruch Spinoza who, unintentionally, offered a philosophical understanding of the cosmos that is similar to that of an oral pagan culture in several aspects. For Spinoza, a body is understood as anything that maintains a collective ratio of motion and rest amongst its constituent elements.[78] A further point that Spinoza makes overlaps nicely with our considerations:

> Bodies are not distinguished in respect of substance. That which constitutes the form of the individual thing consists in a union of bodies. But this union, by hypothesis, is retained in spite of the continuous change of component bodies. Therefore, the individual thing will retain its own nature as before.[79]

While Spinoza is one of the great thinkers of substance ontology, and holds both a totalizing monotheistic view of an absolutely unified universe and a reductive understanding of the nature of things in terms of motion and rest, he hit upon a key idea here. Bodies are defined by patterns of activity, irrespective (and we would say without the need of reference to) either substance or specific constituent bodies. The collective action that is a body is not itself reducible to any more fundamental level; rather, the various things we might seek to discuss in terms of matter, energy, or mind arise from the fundamental level of events or actions.

This is the ultimate philosophical consequence of an oral society's thinking in terms of concrete active descriptions. There is *doing* before we can speak

---

78 While, in other regards, being dramatically monotheistic. This reductive understanding, relying upon the concept of constituent parts and thinking purely in terms of motion and rest, will not be appropriate to the more robust understanding of bodies in pagan culture.

79 Benedictus De Spinoza and Michael L. Morgan, *The Essential Spinoza: Ethics and Related Writings* (Indianapolis: Hackett Pub., 2006), II, Proposition 13, Axiom 3, Lemma 4, Proof.

of *doers*, there are *actions* before we can talk of the *actors* or the objects of actions. Indeed, the entire subject/object model of thought is derivative from more basic events from which the distinction between actor and acted-upon arise.[80] This ties into our earlier arguments against the modern prejudice of viewing humanity in terms of consciousness. Consciousness is the lynchpin of a view of human nature which isolates us from the world in which we exist, and is founded on the visual model, an artifact of writing and the cognitive influence writing has on us. We think of consciousness as something like a gaze, a look that distinguishes the thing looked at and the thing looking. The conscious thing is clearly distinguished from the content of conscious experience.

Consider attempting this type of distinction in a model of experience based on taste. It is clear that we can only taste what we take into ourselves and what becomes part of us. This is knowledge as union, not awareness. Consider also thinking in terms of touch. Notice, for example, that touch is another model of union that undermines the atomistic assumptions of consciousness. Now imagine touch and taste as one, taste as a type of touch and touch as a variety of taste, and we begin to see the sense in which what we become aware of occurs through our union with it. We know by becoming part of the event we would know about, by making that event part of us. This is a participatory model of knowledge. To know, to come to know, is to become-part-of.

More than this, we are always-already part of the world we live through and in. Various movements and actions of knowing involve different unions and disconnections amongst the things that surround us, include us, and are included within us. This may at first sound rather odd and confusing, but remember that the self is not unified and singular within the high pagan worldview. Not only are "we" constantly changing, but we are also plural. Different parts of myself can become aware of different things, unite with different things, while others disconnect from them, and so on. This is reflected in the nature of names in a pagan context. The gods have many names, not one true name. The same can be said for people: it is very common in most pagan cultures for people to take on and leave behind names as they pass through important events; there is not, however, a search for the one true name or identity of a person.

---

80 For a brilliant discussion of this point and what I would consider a relational event ontology generally as it applies to contemporary physics see Karen Barad's *Meeting the Universe Halfway: Quantum Physics and the Entanglement of Matter and Meaning.*

Within pagan metaphysics there is no ruling "I," "consciousness," or "mind" that is (or is not) unified with or aware of anything. Recall Heraclitus: while awake part of me remains asleep and while asleep part of me is dead; I die the life of the gods, while another part of me immortally lives the death of the mortal. I am not one event but am many events, a fact obvious when we consider the nature of the body and its multiple activities and responses. It is only through distortion that we come to prioritize some supposedly consistent one activity we imagine occurs somewhere behind the eyes.[81]

Within philosophical circles, a common objection to event ontology is that it fails to clearly and consistently explain the individuality of given things. How do we distinguish the firm boundaries between any one thing and any other? From the viewpoint of a pagan metaphysics this is a strength of this approach. Pagan animism argues that, if all things are living and if death is only a relative term involving a change in types of life, then we can also say that singularity and individuality are also relative terms. For any given set of activities, we can say how something is "one thing" and how, in respect to another set of activities, it is multiple. However, since change is a fundamental fact, each of these singularities is derived from multiplicity and are therefore only temporary and relative

Change and Interpenetration

The event ontology I am proposing captures the original meaning of the term for nature I discussed previously, *phue* (from which *phusis* is derived). *Phue* is naturing, nature understood as a verb, the process of growth and development. It is closely allied to the role played by Eros/desire in Hesiod. Growth comes before there is something (that is, nature) that is understood as growing. Nature, or rather naturing, is an event and a collection of events in the same way that it is a collection of bodies.

This specific example reflects a general tendency in languages that points to a shared event ontology underlying humanity's oldest ways of thinking. In all languages, there is a historical tendency for centrally important nouns to derive first from verbs. We see this in "nature" (both in the Greek and Latin).

---

81   To capture the arbitrary nature of our images of selfhood it is worth considering that for some cultures thought was understood to occur in the stomach, or the heart. It is not at all self-evident that what we are is an intellectual eye hidden in the skull, this is rather just one poetic image that has become particularly dominant.

We also see it in the German term for "essence," *wesen*, which derives from the old German verb *wesan* and proto-German verb *wesana* that means "to remain" or "to tarry." Active verbs pre-date abstract nouns: naturing before nature, essencing before essence. Notice the reflection of this in the English term "being," which directly attests to its gerund form through its -ing suffix. "Being" is a noun derived originally from a verb, "be." The most important words in any language were originally words for actions and events. Only later are they made timeless and stable through abstraction, a move from an original event ontology to later views, usually monotheistic substance ontologies.

Event ontology allows us to understand some of the more challenging paradoxes that arise when we think about the nature of the gods. I have already insisted that the gods are understood to have bodies, and that they are fully this-worldly and not transcendent. Indeed, the more we think from the perspective of a pagan metaphysics, the more meaningless "transcendence" becomes. Any descriptions of the transcendent seem to consist either of purely negative characteristics (not temporal, not material, not imperfect, etc.) or of concepts emptied so fully of their content as to be unacknowledged stand-ins for "nothingness" (perfection, goodness, all-powerful, etc.). The gods, embodied and this-worldly, are not abstract archetypes. They have personality, individuality, and concrete particularity. Further, many of these bodies undergo wide-ranging transformations.

There is another aspect of the gods we haven't talked about yet, namely the way they can inspire, be channeled by, or even possess humans. In pagan cultures when a person embodies a particularly striking characteristic that falls within the domain of a given god, they were frequently understood to have become that god. Sometimes, this is described as the god appearing as the person. Sometimes, the god is described as inspiring or dictating the actions of the person (for example, Athena talking to Odysseus to guide his wisdom while no one else sees or hears her). Sometimes, the god is said to directly enter and possess the person. All of these are attested to in Ancient Greek literature, but nowhere is there a more highly developed expertise on the varieties of relations like these than in African traditional and diasporic religions.

This aspect of the embodied gods makes clear that gods and the rest of the entities that make up the cosmos (especially humanity) are really inter-bodied. We flow in and out of each other, as interweaving ongoing events which mutually define us. Understanding bodies as matrices of relational actions and events helps us to understand how the bodies of the gods can go through the many changes that they do, as well as being able to interpenetrate our own.

Bodies Within Bodies

One specific example of a body of a goddess makes this particularly clear. Consider Gaia. She is the earth. Not the avatar of the earth, not the archetype of the earth, not the spirit or intelligence of the earth, but the earth itself. Gaia has personality and intellect, to be sure, but we garden and farm in her body and build our houses upon her. She is, to draw on Hesiod, the "broad-bo-somed earth."

The earth is a vast complex of activities: decay involving countless microbes, the reproduction and life activity of a million different kinds of hidden creatures, the pushing of pressure and flow of volcanic forces, the seep of water, the holding of roots, the cracking of rocks by ice, the weight of the icecaps bearing down, universes of viruses and bacteria, fungus and lichen spreading, seeds gestating, buried eggs growing, animal burrows bustling with motion, and hidden bones and the oily remains of ancient life breaking down and exchanging chemical components with the rock around them. At the smallest level, the weak and strong forces of the atomic level provide the "all-supporting" might of rock as particles push and pull against each other. At the largest level, the centrifugal force vies with gravity and the movement of the seas.

Beyond this, there are all the forces that act upon the body of the earth: the fall of rain, the heat of the sun, and so on. Ultimately, the activities which are the earth and the activities which contain, impact, and overlap the earth blend to make her who and what she is. All our meanings, thinking and feeling arise from this, our mother, and add to the buzz of thought and personality that she is. Countless other unknown personalities also act out their existence within and through the earth, to say nothing of those of animals and plants.

All of this composes the collective event of meaning that is Gaia, the body-ing forth and living of the earth itself. Like us, this event of meaning is active, aims and drives towards its own concerns and purposes. Also like us, it is not unified into one singular ego, but rather many meanings, many selves, many purposes and many meaningful actions.

Gaia is one of the broadest of the gods and one of the most concretely bodied, which serves to make her both an informative, and confusing, example. Apollo, Odin, or Ceridwen will be a very different matter. Ultimately, they are all ongoing activities of meaning-making which constitute some of the deepest values of their respective cultures. They also extend well beyond the boundaries of those specific cultures. In the same sense that we make meaning through our actions, choices, creations, and ultimate valuing, so too do the gods make meaning.

Ultimately, what we most fully are is this activity of meaning-making and valuing. To be a body is to make meaning and value. In other words, a body is a body to the extent that it acts in ways to pursue some things and avoid others, create some things and destroy others, and so on. Activity is predicated upon the existence of differences amongst things, and it also depends upon and expands these differences. Meaning is the activity of relating, and meaning is also the relations on which we depend in order to make sense of things.

The gods constitute some of these most basic decisions and actions, ongoing events in which we already find ourselves by existing in the world. Consider, in this regard, the nature of "family" or "heritage" or "tradition." These all represent ongoing events of meaning-making, composed of real personalities and also ultimately part of a larger personality we could call family or community itself. These are meanings within which we find ourselves, and meanings which provide some of the basis for our own meaning-making activities. In other words, meaning is both something real we engage with in the world and also something that we can become part of, can contribute to and create ourselves: like bodies within bodies.

FOURTH INTERLUDE
Taliesin and the Permeability of Being

What remains to us of oral Celtic bardic lore shows the key aspects of a pagan metaphysics that we have already discussed: animism, understanding of body, and event ontology. One of the most common aspects of these poems and stories is the theme of transformation and identification with rather surprising non-human things. Thus, in the Irish *Book of Invasions*, the great poet-magician Amairgen uses poetry to calm the seas for the invading Milesians and then claims:

> *I am the wind upon the sea,*
> *I am a wave upon the ocean,*
> *I am the sound of the sea,*
> *I am a stag of seven points,*
> *I am a bull of seven fights,*
> *I am a hawk upon a cliff,*
> *I am a teardrop of the sun,*
> *I am the fairest of blossoms,*
> *I am a boar of boldness,*
> *I am a salmon in a pool,*
> *I am a lake on a plain,*
> *I am the mound of poetry,*
> *I am a word of skill,*
> *I am a battle-waging spear of spoil,*
> *I am a God who fashions fire in the mind.*[82]

---

82   John Matthews, *Taliesin: The Last Celtic Shaman* (Rochester, VT: Inner Traditions, 2002), 55.

This is a striking paratactic hymn to multiplicity. In similar literature, elsewhere we find "I am" statements replaced instead with claims to having been or become. Thus, in the poem "Cad Goddeu" or "The Battle of Trees" the great bard Taliesin claims:

I have been in many shapes
Before I assumed a constant form:
I have been a narrow sword,
A drop in the air,
A shining bright star,
A letter among words
In the book of origins.
I have been lantern light
For a year and a day,
I have been a bridge
Spanning three score rivers.
I have flown as an eagle,
Been a coracle on the sea,
I have been a drop in a shower,
A sword in a hand,
A shield in battle,
A string in a harp.
Nine years in enchantment,
In water, in foam,
I have absorbed fire,
I have been a tree in a covert,
There is nothing of which
I have not been part.[83]

These claims by the great bards of the Celts have been interpreted in various ways. Some have seen in them a surviving tradition of reincarnation. Though several of the poems attributed to Taliesin contain claims to having lived previously as different humans, it is hard to see how reincarnation fully explains one having been "a string in a harp" and the like. Similarly, reincarnation doesn't account for the inconsistency of whether the poet speaks in the present tense, as Amairgen does, or the past tense, as Taliesin usually does. Others have proposed these claims as evidence of a mystical practice amongst the Celts, one which would allow a person to become part of the

---

83 Matthews, *Taliesin*, 296–97.

collective consciousness of all being (including that of "narrow swords" or "drops in the air" and so on). This, however, over-interprets the poems in order to import a foreign concept of disembodied consciousness.

Let us take a step back and think more slowly about the claims in these poems. First, the claims suggest that things such as spears, swords, waves on the sea, drops in the air, strings in harps and so on have lives, otherwise those things could not be lived to begin with. There is a clear animism here, but that animism should not be understood in terms of a modern idea of consciousness distributed amongst all things. Instead, these point to the world as a series of living interconnected events, and we can take part in those events through our own lived, bodily actions (including the bodily actions called thought).

We don't need to appeal to collective mind or spirit to understand the basis of these claims. Rather, the concept of collective life threads together this understanding. When I am lost in the music of the harp, entirely dedicated and lost in perhaps the vibration of one perfect note on one string, I live the life of that string. This is even more the case when I play that harp, or become one with the sword, shield, or spear in the wild war dance. These things live as part of me and I as part of them.

Such an understanding might still allow for something like reincarnation, but the very term is inaccurate since it relies too heavily on the idea of the unified *individual* self. Instead, the event that I have come to be, something constantly changing anyway, was part of previous ongoing lives and will be part of future ones. We are multiple, made of many lives and living towards many lives.

Consider the following selection from "The Battle of the Trees," usually assumed to be about the creation of Blodeuwedd, though sometimes also assumed to be a description of Taliesin himself. For our purposes either interpretation works, for it captures some of what it is to be the multiple living events we, and all things, are:

> *Not of mother nor of father was my creation.*
> *I was made from the ninefold elements—*
> *From fruit trees, from paradisiacal fruit,*
> *From primrose and the hill-flowers,*
> *From the blossom of trees and bushes.*
> *From the roots of the earth was I made,*
> *From the broom and the nettle,*

From the water of the ninth wave.
Math enchanted me before I was made immortal,
From Emrys and Euryon, from Mabon and Modron,
From five fifties of magicians like Math was I made—
Made by the master in his highest ecstasy—
By the wisest of druids was I made before the world began,
And I know the star-knowledge from the beginning of Time.[84]

None of these living-events need to have awareness in the same form that I do: even I do not always have the same type of awareness throughout my life. All these events are living, and there is *something-it-is-like* to live each of them. This something-it-is-like is often over-interpreted in terms of atomistic mind/consciousness/soul; we would do better to avoid these assumptions.

This is all still an incomplete answer, however, and to see why we need to consider Taliesin's origin story. The standard version of Taliesin's origins is that he was originally a boy named Gwion who worked for the sorceress or goddess (or sorcerer-goddess) Ceridwen. Ceridwen wished to brew a potion of wisdom and inspiration for her son; this potion needed to be stirred constantly as it cooked, and this task fell to Gwion. Before the potion could be given to Ceridwen's son, however, one perfect drop of the potion, the full outcome of the work, leapt from the cauldron and fell on Gwion's finger. Burned, the boy sucked his finger to lessen the pain and thus received all of the wisdom and inspiration intended for Ceridwen's own son. When she learned what had happened, Ceridwen became enraged and chased after the boy. Gwion, using his newly acquired wisdom and power, transformed himself into various different forms, a hare, a salmon, a bird, and so on. Ceridwen herself transformed into different forms in pursuit, such as a hunting hound, an otter, and a hawk. Gwion eventually tries to hide as a grain of wheat, and Ceridwen, as a hen, eats him. This results in Ceridwen becoming pregnant with the devoured Gwion, who is reborn from Ceridwen as Taliesin.

Let us look at Taliesin's own telling of this tale in "Taliesin's Song of his Origin," keeping in mind that the seas and bag at the end of the poem are commonly taken to represent the womb:

---

84 Matthews, *Taliesin*, 299.

Firstly I was formed in the shape of a handsome man,
in the hall of Ceridwen in order to be refined.
Although small and modest in my behavior,
I was great in her lofty sanctuary.

While I was held prisoner, sweet inspiration educated me
And laws were imparted me in a speech which had no words;
But I had to flee from the angry, terrible hag
Whose outcry was terrifying.

Since then I have fled in the shape of a crow,
Since then I have fled as a speedy frog,
Since then I have fled with rage in my chains,
—a roe-buck in a dense thicket.

I have fled in the shape of a raven of prophetic speech,
In the shape of satirizing fox,
In the share of a sure swift,
In the shape of a squirrel vainly hiding.

I have fled in the shape of a red deer,
In the shape of iron in a fierce fire,
In the shape of a sword sowing death and disaster,
In the shape of a bull, relentlessly struggling.

I have fled in the shape of a bristly boar in a ravine,
In the shape of a grain of wheat.
I have been taken by the talons of a bird of prey
Which increased until it took the size of foal.

Floating like a boat in its waters,
I was thrown into a dark bag,
And on an endless sea, I was set adrift.

Just as I was suffocating, I had a happy omen,
And the master of the Heavens brought me to liberty.[85]

---

85 Matthews, *Taliesin*, 281.

For a similar presentation of the story we could look to the poem "The Hostile Confederacy" which makes the process of becoming the child of the Ceridwen much clearer:

> *I have been a blue salmon,*
> *I have been a dog, I have been a deer,*
> *I have been a goat on the mountain,*
> *I have been trunk, I have been a beech,*
> *I have been an axe in the hand,*
> *I have been a pin in the tongs.*
>
> *For a year and a half,*
> *I have been a white speckled cock,*
> *Among the hens of Eiddyn.*
> *I have been a stallion at stud,*
> *I have been a battling bull,*
> *I have been a yellow goat.*
>
> *Fecund and nourishing,*
> *I have been a grain discovered*
> *And I have grown on the hill.*
> *The harvester took me*
> *In a corner full of smoke*
> *In order to free my essence.*
>
> *I have been in great suffering;*
> *A red hen took me,*
> *She had red wings and double comb;*
> *I rested nine months*
> *In her belly, as a child.*
> *I have been matured,*
> *I have been offered to the king,*
> *I have been dead, I have been alive,*
> *I have possessed the ivy branch,*
> *I have had an escort;*
> *Before God I have been poor.*[86]

---

86 Matthews, *Taliesin*, 318–19.

There are many variations of this story, not all of them attributed to Taliesin. In the Irish poem, the *Tochmarc Etaine*, the maiden Etaine is transformed into various things by a jealous druidess before finally becoming a butterfly and falling into a glass of wine. She is then drunk by a woman who gives birth to Etaine anew. A similar Irish story in the *Lebor na hudre* tells of Tuan mac Cairill, who transforms into various animals before being eaten by a woman when in salmon form. The women then gives birth to Tuan mac Cairill once more. Both Etaine and Tuan mac Cairill are granted exceptionally long lives due to their transformations and rebirths, and Tuan mac Cairill can also remember, in a manner repeated in Taliesin's poems, the events of most of history as if he were present for them.

While there are certainly lessons here about the continuity of life and concepts of reincarnation (as much as the word itself is inadequate), we need to take these ideas seriously as actual bodily events. Doing so makes clear that these are stories of transforming bodies, not transmigrating souls. This is why the concept of transformation is so important. For the Celts, like most other pagan cultures, transformation from one thing to another, including into grains of wheat or waves on the sea, is taken as a real bodily potentiality.

We see this in the stories of the two nephews of the great magician and king (or god) Math, as told in the *Mabinogion*. Gwydion and Gilfaethwy worked together to rape one of Math's servants. Math as punishment repeatedly transforms them into animals, one male and one female, and they are not transformed back until they bear a child together in each form. Thus, they become a male and female deer, a male and female pig, and a male and female wolf; each time they must remain in those forms until they together give birth to a child that Math transforms into a human. Finally, after these three transformations (each of which took a year to complete), the nephews are allowed to become human once more.

These punishments do not just teach them each what it is like to be other-than-human, but they also teach what it is like to be female, pregnant, and a mother. The spectrum of transformations open in a pagan culture absolutely includes transformations of gender. More so, the fundamental importance of transformation, and the seemingly endless spectrum of the transformations possible, undermine any idea of essence or purity. To Taliesin, to Gwydion and Gilfathwy, to Etaine and Tuan mac Cairill, no specific characteristic is essential or necessary. Gender, species, type of thing, even whether one is a thing at all or a part of an event, all of these interpenetrate and transform. The one thing that keeps us the same is the ongoing event that is our "essencing," which is not built on top of a stable "essence."

We should not fall into the trap of taking these stories purely symbolically. As I have stressed previously, pagan poetry is not symbolic but rather aims at concrete literal description. Change and multiplicity are the nature of the cosmos, and so they are also the nature of all the living-events that make up the cosmos.

Thus, within what remains of an oral Celtic tradition, we clearly see an understanding of the cosmos based on irreducible pluralism and limitless change. This is a living reality in which being is fully permeable and all beings interconnect and interpenetrate others. It is a living reality with the open possibility of living very different lives and fully, bodily, becoming them. Taliesin and his fellow Celtic bards offer a vision of wisdom and power based on the pagan metaphysics I have been presenting throughout this text: they have power and wisdom because they have lived the reality of the plurality of events that compose the cosmos.

CHAPTER FIVE
The Honesty of Impurity:
Remainders, Monsters, and Incompleteness

When your metaphysics is based upon unity, reduction, totalizing, and Oneness, your approach to the world will be shaped by it. Your approach to the world will focus on perfection, purity, and the one narrow path to the only acceptable goal. In such a view, each thing has an essence that it either fulfills or betrays. Likewise, each thing has a purpose that it either serves or neglects. Oneness is purity, multiplicity is sin.

This basic point dominates our modern thinking and can be seen in the bones of our languages. Consider, for example, our use of the term "integrity." To have integrity, which nationalism and general ethics alike consistently demand, is to be integrated, to be unified and ruled by the One: to be pure.

The pagan world was not devoid of concepts of purity, but these concepts were contextual and specific, similar to the way we distinguish a dirty dish from a clean one. Absolute purity was meaningless until the rise of Platonism and the idea of the purifying ascent to the One, the *kalos kai agathos*, "the Beautiful and the Good in itself by itself." Before the idea of the immaterial purity of the One, there was no concept of an absolute metaphysical purity. There was also no idea of a purity achievable by a metaphysically singular thing, a thing with a given purpose and essence. The rise of Platonism began the rule of purity and order.

The Politics of Purity

When Platonism became preeminent, and pagan religion in Greece (including the old Greek mystery cults) and elsewhere was reinterpreted in terms of it, distinctions built upon the idea of transcendence dominated and continue to dominate now. These distinctions include that between the Celestial and Chthonic and between Theurgy and Goetia.[87]

What is now a distinction between the purity of the non-material and the impurity of the earthly and physical was originally a distinction between different worldly realms: the sky/Olympus, the earth and sea, and the Underworld. For example, the earliest generations of the gods of Greece, including Gaia and her children the Titans, were associated with the earth and Underworld. The children of Kronos and Zeus' own children, on the other hand, were largely associated with Zeus' rule over the skies from Olympus. These two sets of associations seemed to create a tension between the skies and the earth.

This distinction, however, is as often inaccurate as it is useful. While it represents a cultural tendency to understand *older* forces in terms of the earth and *newer* orders in terms of the heavens, this distinction doesn't apply in many other cases (for instance, Poseidon, Demeter, Artemis, Dionysus). Further, this distinction is still this-worldly; that is, the idea of transcendence that arose from abstract thinking (made possible by writing) is utterly absent from this older distinction.

The ancients often understood the stars and constellations as maps of the Underworld, a fact which undermines our current conceptions of heaven and the heavenly. The sun, identified with Helios, was understood as both heavenly and Underwordly: it passed through the Underworld at night and thus shared its power with both realms. Only with the later rise of Apollo (understood as a sun god rather than his original identification with war and disease) do the sun and Apollo take on a more exclusively heavenly meaning.

The changes in these traditions corresponded with a consolidation of state power through the enforcement of various state religions in an attempt to undermine the power and authority of local cults and magical practitioners. The period of high pagan Archaic Greece, as well as other similar cultures elsewhere in the Mediterranean and Middle East, ended with a collapse of the

---

87 For a presentation of the differences between the Chthonic and Celestial, both in terms of its historical development and its role in recent occult developments, see my "Neo-Chthonia" in *Fenris Wolf* volume 8.

highly multicultural and interconnected Archaic world and the beginning of a widespread "dark age." Greece, in particular, faced total political disintegration from about the time of the fall of Troy (likely in 1184 BC) until the rise of writing and the city-state in the eighth century. During this dark age, social organization was exceptionally tentative, and what we might call religious practice was local and diverse. Those who led those local religious practices fit into something like a natural priesthood: those with natural magical and mystical capabilities, along with those possessing inherited knowledge of healing, herbs, and various charms and magic. Some of these functions would also have been handled by traveling *goets*, something like a cross between a folk healer, magician, and priest. Except in extreme situations, the religious practices of each person fell more on their individual shoulders than those of anyone with a socially recognized religious role.

With the rise of writing and the city state, Greek religion becomes increasingly codified for political purposes. Official priesthoods and cults both arose, and they were protected by the force of law. In order to maintain official priestly classes and cliques, ideas like purity are very useful. Insisting upon various rules of cleanliness, and then extreme taboos against various common behaviors, allows for the majority of people to be kept out of the realm of divine power. This favors those able to explicitly commit their entire lives solely to the pursuit of purity. The most obvious example in the contemporary world involves the rule against Catholic priests marrying or engaging in sexual activity. This largely frees Catholic priests from the threat that everyday people will take up the types of practices over which the Church wishes to maintain a monopoly.

Metaphysical purity based on the immaterial nature of the One had more than religious significance. With its rise came the idea of an order for all of life and society, an order based upon the perfect structure ordained and established by the One. If the universe is seen to be governed by spiritually perfect unity, society becomes seen as either ordered and tyrannically ruled by the divine One's intentions, or diverse and multiple in a manner that can only be viewed as unclean, sinful, and chaotic. We see this in the Christian idea of the divine right of kings, and also the Platonic city with its sharp social classes (each meant to mimic the purity of a virtuous soul and the cosmic order of perfect Forms). Since the rise of monotheistic metaphysics, politics has mostly been the politics of purity: one of the most murderous and disastrous ideas in the history of human existence.

In our contemporary world, we are familiar with the presence and increasing rise of the politics of purity. Nationalism, for instance, defines itself in terms of various national characteristics (often racial-ethnic characteristics, but also linguistic and cultural ones) that capture a national essence. Only "true" members of the nation have these characteristic, and only having these characteristics includes a person as part of the collective. Nationalism also requires its pure members to avoid and reject contamination from extra-national influences and ways of life.

Gender and the Foreign

Unfortunately, pagan cultural and religious aspects have also been used by state forces to help define the national essence they would enforce. Thus, there is a poisonous tendency for those with pagan interests and leanings to commit themselves to nationalist and racist movements, as well as to views of religious and cultural supremacy. The idea becomes that being Greek is important to Greek paganism, or being white to the Norse religion, or being one form or another of British is important to practicing Celtic religion, and so on. But though it is easy enough to find colonial, racist, tyrannical pagan states in history (the Roman Empire is an easy example, as is the slave-state of Sparta or the Athenian Empire), the metaphysics of the cultures within which these governments and nations arose opposed these developments.

Let us return to some basics. There is nothing pure about pagan cosmologies and theologies, and this is true in every possible sphere in which we might discuss purity. The gods are never racially pure, pure in terms of sex or gender, pure in their national or cultural identities, or otherwise.

First, let's consider the Norse pantheon. The rule of Odin and his fellow gods was largely predicated on the outcome of an early war between two different families of gods: the Aesir and Vanir. We know sadly little about this war and the original identity of either the Aesir and Vanir, but what we do know is informative. The Vanir seem to have been largely identified with fertility, the earth and sea, and magic. The Aesir are largely seen as more warlike, and have less immediate identification with natural characteristics. Thus, the conflict between the two families has often been interpreted in terms of a war between different cultures.

Looking at a common term for contemporary practitioners of old Norse paganism, the "Asatru" which denotes one who is committed and true to the Aesir, one would think that the Norse pantheon was based on the triumph of the Aesir over the Vanir. This is not the case. However the actual war ended, the outcome of it was the intermarrying of Aesir and Vanir and the exchange of gods from one family to another. In fact, the ability of the gods to work magic, compose poetry, partake in prophecy and generally experience the power associated with wisdom all largely derive from the peaceful intermingling of Vanir and Aesir. This is to say nothing of the frequent intermixing of the Norse gods with giants, elves, and the like, producing important and powerful children. Indeed, Odin himself is the child of a giant. You would be hard-pressed to find a less racially or culturally pure community than that of the Norse gods, and yet many followers of the Norse overtly commit themselves to racism and some to fascism.

Archeologically, what we find when we look to high pagan oral cultures is that they existed during periods of difficult and complex cultural sharing. Their religious understanding and its underlying metaphysics is informed by this ability to come to terms with difference and otherness through compromise, alliance, intermixing, partial or complete adoption, and so on. There is not, and has never been, a pure culture or race; pagan cultures, unlike many of our own, were overtly aware of this and made it a major theme of their myths and wisdom traditions.

The most fundamental ethical code of Archaic and Classical Greek culture was Greece's "guest code" and the practice of "guest-friendship." In Greece, guests were holy, and anyone seeking hospitality had to safely and graciously be granted it. Zeus was understood to rule over these guest practices and to be a patron god of the stranger.

It bears repeating: strangers and especially foreigners were considered holy and personally protected by Zeus. In fact, the entire *Odyssey* can be interpreted as being about the concept of this guest code by showing different ways in which this code is either respected or broken (for example, by the monstrous Cyclops who rather than feed his guests eats them). Similarly, the most common justification for the Trojan War is not that Paris stole Helen from her husband, but rather that he did so *while a guest in the husband's house.*

We see the same type of guest-code in Norse religion. The wisdom sayings of the *Havamal* are mostly about the necessity of treating guests well and behaving well as a guest. Many of the legends about Odin, like many of the gods, involve him disguising himself as a stranger and traveling about the worlds. One must be careful of foreigners and strangers, for any one of them might be a god, and so the foreigner was to be respected with great care.

We have already mentioned the rather striking point that the Greeks had a god overtly identified with the foreign, with the very concept of Otherness: Dionysus. But here our discussion goes beyond merely the foreign in terms of other cultures and communities, though that is clearly intended in Dionysus' identification as a foreign god by the Greeks (despite his actual historical origins in Greek culture). Dionysus, as a god of intoxication, is the god of our own foreignness, of those moments when we become foreign to ourselves and to those who know us most. When we are not ourselves, when we are out of ourselves in mania, inspiration, intoxication, and madness, we are under the influence of Dionysus. He is the god of the Other, and the god that makes Other.

This otherness even goes so far as to undermine any concept of purity in gender or species. One need only recall Euripides' play *The Bacchae*, in which Dionysus comes as a foreigner to Thebes and inspires the women to run off to the mountain to practice his sacred rites. There the women cross over the lines between the genders and also those between the human and animal, inspired and pushed beyond the limits of their usual social position. This same thing happens when Dionysus, in disguise, inspires the king of Thebes (who opposes the new religious practices) to dress as a woman to go spy on the religious bacchanal. Once dressed as a woman, the king himself begins to feel the madness inspired by Dionysus and begins to perceive that it is the god himself with whom he is speaking. Despite this, the king is unable to sufficiently become one with the ritual to pass over his own limits; instead he is torn apart by the women, including his own mother. His mother remains convinced for a long while that her son was actually a mountain lion, thus underscoring the way in which Dionysus causes the crossing of boundaries. Since the king couldn't become other than himself in the ritual, he becomes other than himself in his death.

Dionysus, like Athena, carries within his own story the undermining of gender distinctions. Athena is born from Zeus' head after Zeus devoured her mother Metis. The ability to take on the characteristic powers of a woman is what allows Zeus to avoid the fate of his father and grandfather, to be overthrown by his son. Instead, Athena, who was meant to be born as a man, is born as a woman with male characteristics because Zeus himself became female to give birth to her. In a similar manner, Zeus gives birth to Dionysus because his mother's request to see Zeus' true form destroys her in the burst of a lightning flash, leaving the premature child in need of being carried within Zeus' own thigh. Athena and Dionysus alike represent the permeability of gender distinctions within the Greek world, and the power that comes from sexual impurity and the ability to pass through the apparent boundaries between the sexes.

From the very beginning the lines between genders are clearly permeable: some of the oldest gods give birth without sexual reproduction. In this regard, it is worth meditating upon the striking description of Hekate, in the *Greek Magical Papyri*, as "self-gendered," while also remembering the instability of both gender and species in the poetry of the Celts. We also shouldn't make the mistake of assuming the dual gender conceptual schema, even with all its permeability, is universally the rule for pagan cultures. There are divinities who fit into neither or both, as well as numerous other ways in which these modes of existence have been understood and divided in non-dualistic ways. Like all other dualisms, this is ultimately more deceptive than informative.

Temporary Orders and the Fragility of Divine Politics

A pagan cosmos is always one in transition. We see this throughout pagan pantheons, which are always partial and incomplete stories. It is clear that while Zeus has postponed his own overthrow, this postponement is tentative and temporary. Odin, similarly, is full of his own knowledge of his future downfall and the rise of future generations of new gods and peoples. Pagan worlds are always in the process of change, always *en media res*, in the middle of the story still being developed and unstoppable, though unpredictable and under-determined.

Monotheism, on the other hand, presents certain essential characteristics of reality as unchangeable and unconquerable while making clear that if history is a story it is one already written and known by the ultimate author. Pagan cosmoses are without ultimate authors. Where monotheism is reductive, paganism is productive and understands the ongoing story of the cosmos as arising from within its elements. Future generations, and future realities, arise from previous existences without totalizing and unchanging governing forces.

An incomplete cosmos of remainders from previous stories, an open-ended cosmos of inevitable change, is one that consists of both hope and responsibility. The living events that constitute the cosmos at any given time are all that can and will give rise to the future. There is no reassurance that things will work out in the end, and no set structure that will keep some universal tyranny in place. Anything can, and eventually will, change.

This tentative nature of order must be kept in mind when we look at the common monarchies that arise within the mythologies of pagan cultures. These are never metaphysically inevitable, unlike the rule of the monotheistic One. They are always late-comer rulers in one way or another, and they are always based upon various complex alliances and temporary agreements. The rule of Odin rests upon the many oaths sworn upon his spear, and the alliances with discontented Titans alone provide Zeus with the lightning bolt and the power to overthrow his father. Whether a monarchy or otherwise, the authority of the political structures of the gods always arises from the community and remains open to renegotiation.

We see this point used by human practitioners in the *Greek Magical Papyri*, where often bargains are made, or threats leveled, based on the human ability to appeal to forces that might endanger the ruling gods. I offered an example of this in Interlude Three, in the second spell in which the magician states that the called deities should do what the magician wants and, in exchange, the magician will preserve the body of Osiris and will not free Typhon. There are other spells in which one threatens Olympian gods with a possible call to Titans. It is undoubtedly audacious for a human to threaten the ruling gods, but it does make clear that rebellion against the gods is not only thinkable but even a practical option in many situations. In light of our previous discussion of Dionysus who overthrows standard boundaries, it is worth recalling that according to some traditions Dionysus was destined to supplant the rule of Zeus.

Empty Perfection and the Monstrous

Monotheism involves an odd oscillation between two different views of the One god, an oscillation made most thematic in Christian thought. The common worshiper is unable to connect with an abstract idea of the "perfect good," while the metaphysics of the religion requires such an inhuman entity. Instead, the religion offers anthropomorphic human-like images of the god: god as the father, god as the suffering young man, god as a child, the human mother who is closest to perfection and can intercede for us, the saints, and so on. In this schema, the human god is theologically inadequate, while the abstract god is psychological inadequate. Christianity covers this problem with the unexplained and unexplainable mystery of the savior as "god and man," but each of the great monotheistic religions has dealt with a similar tension and used various means to address it.

The birth of the philosophy of religion in Plato, or perhaps the Pre-Socratic criticisms of Greek traditional religion, is based first and foremost on the recognition that something "perfect" cannot be human. Abstract perfection and humanity are incompatible. As Plato repeatedly has Socrates insist, the perfect cannot change and cannot be changed by what happens in the world. So, a perfect god cannot listen to or answer prayers, cannot desire or require sacrifice, cannot care about people, and so on. From this we get the most honest presentations of abstract perfection in history, the Platonic abstract Form of the Good and the Aristotelian Unmoved Mover. The Unmoved Mover is particularly informative, as its perfection is predicated upon the fact that it cannot be aware of anything other than itself, because awareness of the changing would itself involve change—even if just change to the content of its awareness.

There are two different and conflicting lessons we can draw from Plato and Aristotle's arguments. They want us to realize that god must be perfect, but then consequentially god cannot be human. Alternatively, one might decide that it was the very idea of the abstract perfection that was mistaken. An older argument against the Greek gods shows up in Xenophanes, who points out in fragment 169 that "if cattle and horses or lions had hands, or were able to draw with their hands and do the works that men can do, horses would draw the forms of the gods like horses, and cattle like cattle, and they would make their bodies such as they each had themselves."[88] In other words, we form the gods in our own image and thus are deceiving ourselves.

The problem with Xenophanes' otherwise very clever criticism is that paganism by and large has not dealt with exclusively anthropomorphic gods. This should have been clear from our previous discussion of the bodies of the gods: although Gaia is given some human-like qualities, in many other ways she is far from anthropomorphic. She is, instead, the name given to the living earth itself. Similarly, the transformative powers of the gods make clear that they are not simply human-like, and their ability to move between common categories of bodily natures, genders, and so on breaks the model of the standard human.

But it clearly goes beyond this: not all gods have even surface resemblanc-

---

88 J. H. Lesher, "Xenophanes of Colophon, Fragments: A Text and Translation with a Commentary" (Toronto: Univ. of Toronto Press), Frag. 15.

es to the human. There are monstrous gods, and gods that embody characteristics of animals. There is the monstrous Typhon who we have already mentioned, the last child of Gaia whose head was said to be a hundred snakes.
There was his mate, Echidna, who was half snake and half woman. There
was the Babylonian Tiamat, a monstrous goddess of chaos who was both the
fertile source of all life and a terrible serpent or dragon. There was the Norse
Ymir, the massive giant out of which the world was crafted. And there is one
of my favorite goddesses, the Egyptian Sekhmet, who takes the form of a
lion-headed woman. She is both a force of protection and healing as well as
a goddess of destruction, war, and disease.[89]

All these goddesses and gods are dangerous, as indeed all divinities are,
but they also can have positive aspects while playing central roles in the history of the cosmos. Without a totalizing or reductive structure, there is no universal standard from which any gods or goddess can be understood as good
or evil. The only question is in what way and to what extent they are useful,
dangerous, granting of wisdom, and so on. It would be a very serious mistake
to assume that the huge spectrum of divine and semi-divine entities within the
pagan cosmos are primarily human at all, even those that might seem so.

It is for this reason that the dead can play such an important role in the
magical and religious practices of pagan cultures. The dead remember what
it is to have been human, and they, more than divinities, are able to be understood by us and more fully and successfully communicated with. Despite
appearances, there will always be an unavoidable aspect of enigma in the
relationship between most gods and humanity. The only limiting factor in this
regard is that we all share in the life of the cosmos and, as pointed out by
Heraclitus, find ourselves in a shared relation to each other through this life.

There is one final example worth considering when contemplating the extent to which pagan entities are not strictly anthropomorphic but instead en-
gender a variety of forms of Otherness. The example I have in mind is that of
the wild varieties of faeries within Celtic cultures. The topic of faeries is rather
challenging for our purposes, as our primary source for them is oral folklore
derived from the modern period. Their connection to previous religious figures
and concepts is highly debated. They have been identified with spirits of the
dead, with the old pagan gods who had been forced literally underground
into burrows in which faeries were supposed to live, with generations of gods

---

89 It was upon facing one of her statues at the Metropolitan Museum of Fine Art that I experienced one of
the most overpowering feelings of awe I have ever felt in my life.

that predated the main gods of the Celts, and during the Christian era with fallen angels, angels who remained neutral during Lucifer's rebellion and so were neither damned nor allowed back to heaven, and several other theories and myths.

What seems consistent, however, is the semi-divine nature of faeries in the sense that they are embodied, exceptionally long-lived or immortal, connected to super-human powers and knowledge, and almost entirely unfamiliar with human forms of morality or concerns. Their nature differs from place to place, from being seen as a positive force that only harms when insulted, to being seen as exceptionally dangerous and primarily threatening to human welfare. They are not consistently formed like humans, either. We have examples such as the Kelpie, Ceffyl Dwr, Each-uisge, etc., a very dangerous water faery who has the form of a horse and carries people away to drown. The faery, Sidhe, Sith or any other name by which they are called resemble humanity most often as a seduction and trap, rather than through any real resemblance to us. Despite that, it is possible for humans to become members of the realms of the faery and for human and faery to interbreed. As in the many other examples we have discussed, in human-faery relations we find both foreign otherness, the truly uncanny, and a shared life on a spectrum of possible lives living into and out of each other.

The Pragmatic and Faith

These considerations should make clear the extent pagan thinking is, in a positive sense, *impure*. This is what it means to embrace the plural and changing. This impurity arises also in the attitude of a pagan culture generally towards its divinities. As already mentioned, Wiredu claims that the Akan society of Ghana has a highly practical and even experimental attitude towards their divinities. The Greeks were very similar. The extent to which the gods aided humanity, or used their power to make clear that they had to be dealt with and/or appeased, determined the extent to which humans gave them attention. Rebellion against the gods was not unthinkable, nor was moving on from gods who no longer proved important, useful, or dangerous if ignored. In other words, the concept of a "test of faith" is exceptionally foreign to the pagan mindset, as is the idea of faith as we have come to understand it now.

The god of monotheism is widely considered to require of its worshipers a "faith in things not seen." In other words, faith requires a commitment to the existence of something that has refused to make itself known in any clear manner. Precisely because a god doesn't show itself, doesn't display its power, doesn't answer prayers in a dependable way or punish blasphemy in a predictable way, this god requires faith.

For most pagans, such a faith would be a fool's game, the opening move of a huge con. If a god refused to show its existence and power, refused to contribute to human life, refused to grant its wisdom or insights to its worshipers, refused in fact to have any intimate relationship with its people, then this god is hardly worth thinking about at all. Such a creature is best left alone, dismissed as a phantom or as a rather unimportant and worthless hypothetical reality. The idea that "thou shalt not test the lord thy god" is, in fact, one of the clearest anti-pagan statements ever made. A wise person absolutely tests their gods, if in a manner appropriate to the deity in question (one should avoid the dangers of giving offense, of course). But worship granted based on vague future promises would seem a rather silly thing to most pagans.

Faith is ultimately about something other than belief: it is about obedience. We see this in all the classic examples of tests of faith. A test of faith is always a provocation to defy or question the god. To pass such a test is to refuse questioning and, instead, to obey. To pursue purity is to maintain faith, to defy purity is disobedience. Within a pagan context, however, obedience is always considered within pragmatic terms. One must surely be obedient in certain situations where to do otherwise would be foolishly dangerous, but obedience in and of itself is not to be valued (rather the reverse, in fact).

Obedience to various gods may frequently be prudent, but it isn't ethically required. Rather, in some cases there are other gods to which one can appeal in opposition to the god one has chosen to defy. In the most extreme cases, general rebellion is always an option, albeit an uncommon one. We see rebellion in the case of Heracles, who frequently works against the will of Zeus. Rebellion is also exemplified in the Titan Prometheus, who rebelled against Zeus' in a way that ultimately resulted in humanity's benefit (though not his own).

In pagan cultures, we have countless stories of gods being tricked by humans, being beaten in competitions and bargains, even being bested in battle. These are the characteristic actions of heroes. The closer humanity approaches to divinity, in its heroic characteristics for example, the more rebellious and disobedient it tends to become. This is precisely as it should be, since the gods themselves often conflict and rebel one against another.

The implications of this should be clear for politics. Politics of purity have no place within a pagan worldview; likewise, concepts of obedience are also highly suspicious. The idea of obedience without question, of respect for authority simply as authority without justification and the possibility of critique, derives inevitably from the monotheist's subservience to some One Ultimate tyrannical Good. Things must be worthy of respect to be respected, and to be worthy of respect a thing must demonstrate its value rather than propose "tests of faith" and demand obedience. In this sense, from a pagan view, the only appropriate response to a test of faith is to fail it. It is the divinity, and any other source of supposed authority, that is to be tested.

FIFTH INTERLUDE
The Eleusinian Rebellion

*But grief yet more terrible and savage came into the heart of Demeter,
and thereafter she was so angered with the dark-clouded Son of Cronos
that she avoided the gathering of the gods and high Olympus, and went to
the towns and rich fields of men, disfiguring her form a long while. And
no one of men or deep-bosomed women knew her when they saw her,
until she came to the house of wise Celeus who was then lord of fragrant
Eleusis.*[90]

Rebellion against the gods, playing one god off against another, leveling
threats against divinities, and taking a stand in godly conflicts are all well
attested to in pagan magical practices as preserved in documents such as *The
Greek Magical Papyri.* In one striking example from the papyri the magician
threatens to bind Adonis permanently in the underworld unless Aphrodite
fulfills a demand:

*But, if as goddess you in slowness act,
You will not see Adonis rise from Hades,
Straightway I'll run and bind him with steel chains;
As guard, I'll bind on him another wheel
Of Ixion, no longer will he come
To light, and he'll be chastized and subdued.*[91]

---

90 Hesiod and Hugh G. Evelyn-White, *Homeric Hymns. Epic Cycle. Homerica* (Cambridge, MA: Harvard
University Press, 1936), lines 90–97.
91 PGM IV 2902–07.

The Roman poet Lucan gives us an even more dramatic example in his *Pharsalia*, where a witch launches into dramatic threats against the underworld gods unless they send to her a specific spirit she desires to speak with:

> *Tisiphone and Megaera, you who scorn my calling, do you not drive this hapless soul through the emptiness of Erebus with your cruel whips? Any moment now I shall call you up by your names and make you stand as Stygian hounds in the light of the upper world. I shall pursue you through tombs, through burials, ever hanging on your heels, I shall drive you from barrows and keep you from all urns. You, Hecate, decaying and colourless in appearance as you are, are in the habit of showing yourself to the gods above only after first making up your face. I will show you to them and forbid you to alter your hell-face. I shall blurt out, Persephone of Henna, the meal that traps you beneath the vast weight of the earth, the agreement by which you love the sombre king of the night and the corruption you experienced that induced your mother to refuse to call you back. Upon you, Hades, worst of the world's rulers, I shall send Titan, the Sun, bursting your caverns open, and you will be blasted by the instantaneous light of day. Do you obey?*[92]

Indeed, as our earlier discussion of *The Oresteia* should make clear, in a cosmos of diverse gods in conflict, siding with any gods will ultimately consist in rebelling against others. Magicians have always made the most of these conflicts, leveraging them for their own freedom and empowerment. This negotiable relationship to divinities (and amongst divinities) is an inherent element of paganism for metaphysical and theological reasons.

One could argue, however, that the itinerant magician or witch might not be the best representative of the worldview from which they take their origin. Anticipating this objection, it might be useful to show a more official cultural practice that displays the leveraging of conflict amongst the gods for the benefit and empowerment of humans. Luckily, a beautiful and perfect example is available to us in the famous Eleusinian Mysteries.

The Eleusinian Mysteries were an initiatory religious mystery cult in Ancient Greece, open at its peak to anyone irrespective of social status. What we know about the mysteries is fairly limited, but we have a pretty clear picture of their mythological background and intended goal, as well as some

---

92 Lucan and Jane Wilson Joyce, *Pharsalia* (Ithaca: Cornell Univ. Press, 1993), 6.642. Thanks to Kim Huggens for her paper "The Truth about Zombies, or: How to Survive the Zombie Apocalypse" in the excellent collection *Memento Mori: A Collection of Magickal and Mythological Perspectives on Death, Dying, Mortality and Beyond* which first drew my attention to this passage.

of their specific ritual components.[93] Our main knowledge of the mysteries is drawn from the "Homeric Hymn to Demeter" and surviving sculptures and paintings depicting aspects of the rites. The mythological background of the mysteries is depicted in the Hymn: Persephone's abduction by Hades with the consent of Zeus, and Demeter's search for her daughter and rage in response to the events. We are also aware that the mysteries likely provided the initiates with good fortune while alive and a happier afterlife than that experienced by most shades in the underworld.

There were two stages to the mysteries, the first performed in Athens and the second performed in the city of Eleusis. We are fairly certain that the mysteries involved Demeter's search for Persephone, the consumption of the meal and pennyroyal drink that Demeter drank while in self-imposed exile from Olympus, and the use of torches and fire to purify the initiate. It is my suspicion that the mysteries also featured Hekate in a central role, which would account for the goddess' centrality in the "Hymn to Demeter": she is key to Demeter's uncovering of the abduction. Hecate is also presented as always going both before and after Persephone from thence onward, marking her as a goddess of both the land of the living and land of the dead.

The city of Eleusis, the central location of the mysteries, features in the "Hymn to Demeter" as the place where Demeter went when enraged with Zeus and Hades. It was also during this period that she withdrew her blessing from the earth and blighted the world's crops. Here we have one of the most famous conflicts amongst the gods, one that threatened the balance of the entire cosmos. One way to think about this conflict is that it was between the forces of death represented by Hades, king of the underworld, and the forces of life represented by Demeter goddess of the earth (and specifically growing things and agriculture). More than this, it was also a conflict between Demeter and Zeus, who allowed for Persephone's abduction.

Demeter's response to this betrayal on the part of the official authority of Olympus and Hades is to seek to usurp and undermine the authority of Hades himself. She seeks to usurp the power of death by blighting the earth, thus becoming a force of death herself. More interestingly, she seeks to undermine the power of death during her time in Eleusis. While there in disguise she becomes a nursemaid for a young child, Demophoon, and seeks to

---

93 This chapter is particularly indebted to Caroline Tully's excellent investigation of the Eleusinian Mysteries in her paper "Demeter's Wrath: How the Eleusinian Mysteries Attempted to Cheat Death" in *Memento Mori: A Collection of Magickal and Mythological Perspectives on Death, Dying, Mortality and Beyond.*

make him immortal by feeding him ambrosia and having him sleep amidst the flames of the hearth at night. As Catherine Tully puts it,

> One interpretation of her action is that it was a way of gaining revenge on Hades and Zeus for the abduction of Persephone. Just as Hades withholds Persephone from her mother and the upper world, so Demeter attempts to withhold Demophoon from the lower world by making him "deathless." Had she been successful in this initial experiment, she may have gone on to immortalize all humans thus depriving Hades of his rightful honours and seriously disturbing the order of the universe as ordained by Zeus.[94]

Despite her attempt, she is caught placing the child amidst the flames and its mother panics, disrupting the process and depriving her child of immortality. It is for this reason that the mysteries were not able to provide actual immortality but were able to grant a blessed afterlife, an afterlife distinguished by the ability to maintain one's personality rather than becoming a hungry sorrowing shade.

Following the disruption of her plan to provide mortals with immortality, the rageful Demeter demands a temple be built for her at Eleusis in repayment for the way in which she had been doubted by Demophoon's mother. Once completed, "dark-cloaked Demeter" set herself in anger and sorrow within the temple and brought a year of desolation and death upon the earth. Zeus sent, one after another, the various gods to plead with Demeter to relent and to promise her any gift or power she wished amongst the deathless gods. Demeter was unrelenting until finally Zeus arranged for Persephone to be freed from Hades for a portion of the year.

What we should stress here is that Demeter stages a single person revolution against the divine order put in place following the overthrow of Cronos and the rise of the Olympian gods. Against the division of powers put in place by Zeus, Hades, and Poseidon, Demeter stands alone and threatens to either abolish death or bring death to the entire world. Demeter's rebellion succeeds, and results in the compromise which brings us the differences between the seasons, while making both Demeter and Persephone, formerly goddesses of life, goddesses of death as well.

It is Demeter's rebellion that results in the Eleusinian Mysteries with its benefits for humanity. The Eleusinian Mysteries enshrine the power of re-

---

94   Tully, "Demeter's Wrath."

bellion and resistance within paganism, in contrast to the obedience much more representative of monotheism and monotheistically influenced reconstructions of paganism. Just as importantly, the mysteries were not some fringe practice such as might be enshrined in the practices of magicians as documented in surviving papyri and the reports of poets. The Eleusinian Mysteries were exceptionally important to Greek mainstream religion and were respected and protected by official state and religious powers.

Nowhere do we see the importance of the mysteries and their protection by official authorities more clearly than in the story of Alcibiades. Alcibiades is one of the ultimate "bad boys" of history. He was the child of one of the most important and rich aristocratic families in Athens, the nephew of the great statesmen Pericles, and the close friend and sometime student of Socrates. During the war between Athens and Sparta, he repeatedly changed sides and become a symbol of cunning and betrayal.

Alcibiades' first betrayal was provoked by the charge of having profaned the Eleusinian Mysteries during a drinking party. This was a serious enough charge that it would be taken up by a formal Athenian court. Before he could stand trial, however, he was sent away to fulfill his duties as a general in the war against Sparta. While away he was tried in absentia, found guilty, and condemned to death. When recalled from the war to face the death penalty at home, Alcibiades decided instead to defect to Sparta. The Eleusinian Mysteries were an important enough aspect of official and mainstream Greek religious practice for their profanation to result in a death penalty for one of Athens' most powerful and promising young leaders.

The Eleusinian Mysteries, which enshrined the power of rebellion against the Olympian order, were a central aspect of Greek paganism. The extent to which the Eleusinian Mysteries subvert established power and cosmic order cannot be overstated. Demeter rages against the order of the heavens and the underworld, and as a goddess of life she takes on the power and mantle of death, alternating between attempts to abolish death and to make it absolute. It is this fundamental destabilization and subversion that grants the mysteries their power. They represent a fracture in the order of the established cosmos. It is a central insight of paganism that this fracture, these inevitable contradictions in the pluralistic nature of the reality, can be implemented for the benefit and empowerment of humanity amongst the powers of the cosmos. Once again, we find obedience undermined by the potent plurality of realities.

CHAPTER SIX
Nature's Rights[*]

All, and only, humans have rights.[95]

To give preference to the life of a being simply because that being is a member of our species would put us in the same position as racists who give preference to those who are members of their race.[96]

Mother Earth and all its components, including human communities, are entitled to all the inherent rights recognized in this Law. The exercise of the rights of Mother Earth will take into account the specificities and particularities of its various components. The rights under this Act shall not limit the existence of other rights of Mother Earth.[97]

Our understanding of what we mean by "rights" is a mess. There are few topics more important for political discourse, yet no topic is as murky and confused in our thinking. In fact, we don't have much of a grasp at all about what a right is or where it comes from. The pagan metaphysics we have been developing, however, can bring surprising illumination to this problem.

The murky nature of rights talk can be demonstrated fairly easily. Take a moment and attempt to explain to yourself directly what rights exist, where they come from, who has them and why only those (neither more nor less) exist.

---

[*] This chapter is largely drawn from an essay of the same title published in *A Beautiful Resistance: Everything We Already Are.*

95 Carl Cohen's view as presented by Tom Regan, *Animal Rights, Human Wrongs: An Introduction to Moral Philosophy* (Lanham, MD: Rowman & Littlefield, 2003), 112.

96 Peter Singer, Practical Ethics (Cambridge: Cambridge University Press, 2017).

97 *Law of Mother Nature*, Article 5, Bolivian Law.

Or, consider for a moment the seemingly interminable arguments that immediately occur whenever the question of a right's existence or non-existence comes up. Can you offer a clear and applicable principle that allows you to determine real from false rights?

The Political and Natural

Rights can be divided into various categories, some easier to address than others. I will rely upon two fairly simple categories, though others can be offered and this apparent simplicity covers over some deep problems. Rights, for our purposes, can be natural (or Universal, or Implicit, or Inalienable) or legal. Natural rights are understood to exist in any context, free of any political framework or foundation, and are thus found everywhere despite temporal, cultural, or political differences. In turn, these natural rights are understood to legitimize political systems.

Legal rights, on the other hand, depend upon various political and legal structures for their existence. To offer a fairly simple example, life (or human life) is a fairly noncontroversial natural right, while the right to trial by jury is a legal right. Trial by jury cannot exist without a functioning political framework, and we could imagine other social forms to fulfill the legitimate demands of justice other than trial by jury (for instance, trial by council, mediator, or king). However, trial by jury is a social and legal framework, justified by its fulfillment of the demand offered by certain natural rights. That is, the natural rights of life and liberty are supposedly insured by the right to trial by jury, and so these natural rights provide the argument for the legal rights. Thus, legal rights are socially and historically contingent, but legitimated by natural rights that are not contingent.

We can see how the reliance of legal rights on natural rights functions by looking at key rulings by the Supreme Court of the United States of America. The ruling legalizing abortion ("Roe vs. Wade") justifies the legal right to abortion by appeal to the "right to privacy," which in turn is understood as a subset of the natural right of liberty. The recent ruling legalizing marriage equality in all fifty states ("Obergefell vs. Hodges") bases a right to marriage on various other rights such as self-expression which, again, tie back to the basic natural right of liberty.

We can sometimes feel like we have a pretty good grasp on what is and is not a right because many of our legal rights are clearly delineated in political documents and processes. But this is hardly sufficient, especially since rights talk comes up most frequently when we are trying to address cases of systematic injustice in which the existing political framework appears to have failed in some way. Therefore, the most powerful and important grounds are where natural rights connect to and justify legal rights, which is also the territory most fought over. For example, people have argued for years following "Roe vs. Wade" that there is no right to privacy and thus no right to abortion. Justice Scalia, in response to the recent marriage equality ruling, argued that there is no right to self-expression and thus no right to marriage.

Allow me to offer one further example of the contested connection between legal and natural rights. You can find arguments that there is a right to education and a right to healthcare (rights, in turn, vehemently rejected by others). The argument in favor of these rights relies most often on natural rights. The rights to life and liberty are meaningless when one is dying of a curable disease, or when one lacks the necessary education to make meaningful and effective choices in one's own life or in the political processes of one's community.

So, of the flood of rights mentioned above (privacy, abortion, self-expression, marriage, healthcare, education), which do or do not exist, and why? This is a difficult enough question when we consider legal rights, or rights seemingly existing between nature and the law (privacy and self-expression for example), but things get worse when we go to the heart of the issue and ask which specific natural rights exist, why they exist, and where these rights come from.

A History of Rights

Our real focus is natural rights. The ultimate question is drawn from the quotation with which I opened this chapter. We must ask, "Do only humans have rights?" Or, just as Ecuador and Bolivia have enshrined in their legal systems, we must also ask, "does the earth itself have natural inalienable rights?" These questions must also include the narrower question of whether animals have rights, though we must also be just as interested in the question of the rights of plants, environments, mountains, seas, and so on.

To figure out what natural rights do or do not exist, and who or what can be a rights-bearer, we need to determine where these natural rights come from. The history of the concept of natural rights, at least in Western European thought from which most rights talk draws its foundation, stretches from the Ancient Stoics, through medieval religious thought, to the modern social contract theorists such as John Locke, Jean Jacques Rousseau, Thomas Hutchinson, and Thomas Hobbes. Within this tradition, we can find roughly four answers to the question of the origin of natural rights, as well as various ways of testing whether something is a right. Frequently, these answers overlap in complex ways, and looking briefly at each will show their inadequacy.

1. Reason as Natural Law

The Stoics never actually argued for the existence of natural "rights," but they did argue for the natural equality of all humans. Their argument rested on several key elements. First, all nature was understood to be ordered according to an overarching order or law. Second, this law was divine and was identified as reason. Third, human reason was a privileged part of this divine natural order: in fact, reason made us partially divine.

This line of thought leads to two related conclusions. First, to the extent that we have reason, we are equal. This is the origin of the idea that natural rights are inalienable (in other words, we can very literally never lose them). If you reflect on the idea of inalienability, you can see it is a rather odd idea. Can't I be chained up? Or killed? Don't I lose my rights in these cases? The answer in this conception is "no." For the Stoics, and the "inalienable" tradition that follows from them, as long as we can reason, we are ultimately free. Even if my body is in chains, the most important part of me (my divine reason) is free.[98] Because what matters in this view is reason, nothing social inequality does to us can possibly touch our real freedom and equality. Many of the Stoics, as you might suspect, were conservative in the outcome of their thought.

The second conclusion to be drawn from the Stoic view is that the source of our knowledge of rights is also reason. This hooks up with inalienability to provide us with a test that can be applied to rights: if you think something is a natural right, ask whether it is inalienable; if it isn't, you have no right to it. In other words, nothing worth having can be lost, and nothing we have a right to can be taken away. This view is obviously anthropocentric, and even falls short of providing rights to all humans, since some lack reason. For the

---

98 This, incidentally, provides the basis for some Stoics to actually support slavery and social inequalities of all sorts.

Stoics, only humans (but not all humans) have rights, as well as gods and any other entities with reason.

The development of these ideas leads to what we find in Locke and Thomas Jefferson: natural rights are inalienable and uncovered by reason. Both reject the Stoic test as too limited, and instead rely upon the self-evidence of rights. In other words, we don't need a test for what counts as a right, because our natural rights are immediately apparent and obvious to the view of reason. Jefferson doesn't try to prove we have natural rights, he claims he doesn't need to. This has largely landed us in the mess we are in today, with generally no system for determining what is or is not a right. Jefferson and Locke also change the sense of inalienability used by the Stoics. For them, a natural right is inalienable because even if the practice of that right is taken away, our claim to that right always remains. We always deserve and can demand life and liberty even when we are deprived of the use of them.

2. God

The Stoics, Locke, and Jefferson, as well as the long medieval tradition of natural law theory, all base the origin of rights on a certain conception of the divine. This conception is ultimately monotheistic (the Stoics believed in one ultimate divinity despite the existence of sub-deities) and anthropocentric (humans occupy a special position at the head of nature due to our possession of reason and/or special selection by god).

It is important to stress that contemporary rights theory goes beyond the basis of god in very specific ways. First, natural rights do not rely upon a shared religious background for justification. Second, neither the Stoic nor Biblical god provides a basis for rejecting the social inequality of men and women or the practice of slavery. The Bible clearly supports slavery. In fact, the New Testament, which was heavily influenced by Stoic thought, offers arguments in favor of slavery very similar to those found in Stoicism. Most go something like this: social distinctions are natural and divinely willed, so it is our duty to rationally fulfill the social roles and positions we find ourselves in, including the role of a slave. This allows both Stoics and the Biblical Paul to assert that a good slave must obey its master. Locke followed the monotheistic reasoning underlying natural rights rather carefully, arguing from this basis in favor of both American slavery and the wholesale theft of land from the Native Americans.

Finally, it should be noted that the longest use of divinely-ensured natural rights was to support the divine right of kings and firm social hierarchies. This shouldn't be surprising. I have often challenged my students to explain to me why a monarchical metaphysics with a divine all-powerful dictator should be compatible with anything other than a form of political tyranny. It's a difficult question to answer.

3. Nature

Interestingly, the history of natural rights theory hasn't been particularly focused on nature. Nature has seemed to require the underwriting of "nature's god" and/or reason. Despite that, we can detach something of an argument-from-nature from natural rights literature. We can derive from the thought of both Locke and Hobbes a principle for deriving from nature a list of rights. Rights would be, on this reading, those things which a living entity naturally feels are its own. So, in nature we fight for our life, our freedom of movement, our family, and things like food and shelter that we have gathered for ourselves. Our instinctive defense of these things marks a natural knowledge of a right to them.

From a traditional view, the failing of this thinking is obvious: it doesn't set humans off from animals who also defend all these things. For this precise reason, this is more promising for us. Locke, deprived of his Biblical god and the superiority of reason, would be left with an argument like this alone. This can be expanded into a capabilities view, similar to that of the contemporary philosopher Martha Nussbaum,[99] that might assert that a natural entity has a right to develop its natural capabilities. To paraphrase Nussbaum, our sheer having of capabilities is a signal of a right to them and their expression/development.

4. Pain and Pleasure: Utilitarianism

Strictly speaking, Utilitarians don't accept the existence of natural rights for various reasons, but we can talk of something very similar to a rights conception in Utilitarianism based on a limited type of capabilities view. For the utilitarian theorist, only one thing is absolutely good: pleasure or happiness;

---

99 See, for example, Marth Nussbaum's *Creating Capabilities: The Human Development Approach.*

and only one thing is absolutely bad: pain. This lays a universal obligation upon us to increase, as far as possible, the amount of pleasure or happiness in existence and to decrease the amount of pain.

This is the basis of the argument by Peter Singer, perhaps the most famous ethicist currently living, quoted at the start of this chapter.[100] Animals, as capable of pain and pleasure, are part of our obligation to lessen pain and increase pleasure, and might be said to have a right to this type of consideration. Animals have a right to have their suffering and happiness taken into account. Plants, mountains, seas, and so on are not obviously capable of pain or happiness, and so do not enter into consideration beyond their instrumental relationship to animals and humanity.

5. No Natural Rights

We can conclude with a brief consideration of the view that there are no natural rights. If we understand a right to mark a limit, a space or possession that cannot legitimately be invaded or taken away, then the following three views might be raised. Rousseau suggests that since the state of nature is one of natural abundance and simplicity, no natural limits between people in nature exist nor need to exist. Society (which gives rise to pride and greed) creates property, scarcity, and domination, and therefore society makes rights necessary. Hobbes argues something like the reverse: in the state of nature all entities have the power to do whatever they wish, and so they also have the right to do so. Because all action is a natural right for Hobbes, it makes no difference to say that there are no natural rights or that everything is a natural right. This leads to Hobbes' famous "war of all against all" in the state of nature.[101] Finally, since the utilitarian thinks that we must balance the good of the greatest number of entities capable of happiness against any individual concerns, there are no predetermined limits protecting the life, liberty, capabilities, or goods of any given individual. The majority, the "greatest number," might be said to have rights but no given individual does.

---

100 See, for example, Peter Singer's *Animal Liberation.*

101 See, for example, Hobbes' *De Cive* Chapter One section 10: "Nature hath given to every one a right to all. That is it was lawfull for every man in the bare state of nature, or before such time as men had engag'd themselves by any Covenants, or Bonds, to doe what hee would, and against whom he thought fit, and to possesse, use, and enjoy all what he would, or could get." Section 12: "It cannot be deny'd but that the naturall state of men, before they entr'd into Society, was a meer War, and that not simply, but a War of all men, against all men."

To summarize the various views of this last conception: either rights depend on scarcity and since there is no natural scarcity there are no natural rights; or, rights depend on power and, since we naturally have the power to do anything we are capable of, there are no natural limits represented by rights; or, finally, rights belong only to the entity of greatest ethical concern, and since individuals are only instrumentally important in comparison to the whole, the whole might have rights but individuals do not.

Restoring the "Nature" in Natural Rights

How can a pagan perspective assist us in the challenge of making sense of the origin, nature, and limits of rights? We don't have many historical precursors to work with. Clearly much of pagan history hasn't been particularly promising when it comes to individual freedoms or social equality, with rather important exceptions such as many Native American and traditional African cultures. Our strongest precursor might be taken to be the Stoics, but they arguably do not fit into a high pagan worldview. Rather, they represent late paganism with a monotheistic metaphysics. So, we can't really ask what pagans have historically had to say about rights. Instead, we must take key elements of several forms of paganism and attempt to work out their implications for natural rights theory.

The first thing we might note deals with the traditional derivation of natural rights from reason and god. The nature of the god in question leads almost inevitably to the focus on reason. For the Stoic, the ultimate god and reason are all but indiscernible. In fact, the Stoics often called the universal divinity, universal law, and human reason all by the same Greek word: *logos*. *Logos* is originally the Greek term for "word," but it came also to mean "reason" amongst many other things. The Old Testament of the Bible reflects a similar view, whether through syncretism or chance, and the New Testament directly plagiarizes from the Stoic view. In the Old Testament, the god of the Bible speaks creation into existence and the "Gospel of John" starts with an almost entirely Stoic claim that "In the beginning was the *logos*, and the *logos* was with God, and the *logos* was God." In this context, the divine essence of reality will be located in the intellectual, rational, and linguistic spheres of existence. This is also connected to the transcendent nature of a divinity external to creation, a transcendence that will frequently carry over into the rational part of humanity through a rejection of the body and of physical nature in general.

The focus on reason and linguistic communities embodied in the natural rights tradition makes a very clear appearance in contemporary arguments about what can and cannot be a bearer of rights. For an example we might turn to Carl Cohen, a contemporary ethicist and philosopher as well as a long-standing opponent of animal rights arguments.[102] Cohen claims that having a right means being able to assert a claim upon others while recognizing your own obligation to respond to their claims. In other words, only members of rational linguistic "moral communities" can be understood to have rights. Cohen's claim is that only humans can make rational moral claims upon others and recognize those claims when they are made upon them. In other words, whether or not something has rights (and what those rights are) has everything to do with intellectual and linguistic capabilities.

In sharp contrast, consider the pagan worldview of Hesiod's *Theogony*. As previously discussed, in Hesiod the cosmos arises out of the sexual and asexual bodily reproduction of families of gods. These gods, and the evolving universe they form through their reproduction, are inseparable from bodily nature. Importantly, there is a deep identity between nature and its divinities. To appreciate the importance of this, ask yourself whether the Biblical god can be understood to have rights. It's an odd question because the answer is that the god of the Bible probably has all rights (or, rather, absolute right).

What would this imply, then, for the rights of a natural world made up of gods in ever more various proportions and hierarchies? To cultures for which the divine is embodied and natural, rather than spiritually transcendent over nature, the world around us makes constant demands upon us in a manner very like the way traditional rights bearers do. Rivers, mountains, ancient trees, and unplowed fields each make legitimate demands for various types of respect.

A pagan theory of rights, then, will not be focused upon reason or on a divine law-giver's demands upon a tightly structured cosmic hierarchy. The hierarchy of divinities, cosmic forces, and realities within the pagan worldview are temporary and political in nature. Zeus, for example, plots and fights both to gain his position and to maintain it. But even his power is tentative, maintained by the overall balance of politics amidst divinities and humans.

The overlap of nature and divinity in a pagan view presents a unique opportunity: we can turn to nature for guidance about the origin and extent of natural rights. Further, though our pagan worldview might direct our attention

---

102 See, for example, Karl Cohen's book *The Animal Rights Debate*.

to nature, we need not depend upon divine revelation or dictate for our understanding of rights. Paganism might teach us that nature is divine and lays demands upon us, but a pagan faith is not necessary to accept the conclusions we can draw from this. This is particularly true because the metaphysics we have been developing from a pagan theology can be argued for on a purely metaphysical, historical, and linguistic level without the need to draw on any aspect of religious faith.

Paganism conceives the cosmos and all its subsystems (from planets to seas to mountains and so on) to be living, much as the Bolivian "Law of Mother Earth" does. We can add to and clarify our earlier presentation of this animism with the capabilities view of Nussbaum. We start with animals and plants, recognizing that each has a set of capabilities and impulses they seek to express and fulfill. Each thing has an implicit right to pursue the path of its growth, life, and death. To put it as simply as possible, each thing taken in isolation has a right to exist. But, despite the tendency towards what we might call biological chauvinism, organic entities are not the only things which express a nature and follow a path of development and change. All things individually express a type of nature and, collectively, take part in nestled interdependent systems.

There is a Zen art dedicated to finding and appreciating examples of "perfect" stones, stones which best capture the nature of being a stone. These won't be polished gems or dramatic outcroppings, but rather simple stones that somehow express in an exemplary way the basic nature of being a stone. While any debate about what this nature is might be interminable, just like debates about the ultimate nature of humanity, nonetheless it doesn't seem absurd to attempt to better grasp what the nature expressed by stones (or any other natural entity) might be. And it also doesn't seem absurd to suggest that when such a stone is ground into gravel or melted for industrial purposes, something has been lost and some wrong may have been done.

When I was a child, my neighbors cut down an oak tree that had lived for several centuries. I cried inconsolably, filled with a sadness and anger that told me at a basic level that something terrible had been done, an important obligation had been broken, and an important good had been destroyed. Who were they to so casually dismiss an entity that was old before their ancestors had even come to this country? I once went hiking in Prairie Creek Redwood State Park and there, amidst trees that were massive before the supposed birth of Christ, one can't help but feel an overpowering awe and need for respect and even worship. Not only do these entities have a right to exist, they have a dignity that goes along with an imperative that this be respected.

A Pagan Theory of Rights

While we often think about rights in terms of purely negative limits on the powers of others, rights go along with responsibilities and obligations. A right to life or liberty demands that I respect these same rights in others. More than this, a right to life or liberty also lays an obligation on my shoulders to facilitate the living and freedom of others. It is not, as many libertarians might think, purely a right to be left alone and let everyone else alone in turn. Rights are expressions of communal membership, of being part of a dynamic system seeking to further its own development. Rights are the mark of our position in an environment, in nature. The right that I have to my existence and self-development is mirrored in my obligation to protect and pursue the existence and self-development of the world and cosmos of which I form a part.

To restate the previous points in a more schematic form for the sake of clarity: Informed by paganism, but without need to rely upon it for justification, we see that:

1. To the extent that animals fight for their lives and development, they express a right to existence and self-expression.
2. Plants, similarly, strive to grow and survive, expressing the same right.
3. Even non-biological entities are self-sustaining systems that resist certain changes. Also, when they change they change in a manner uniquely expressing their nature; so they, too, express a right to existence and self-expression.
4. Collectively, these elements form larger complex systems that, in turn, strive to change in various ways and resist other changes, and so they express the same natural claim to rights.
5. These rights are nestled, one within another, and are interconnected such that no purely individual atomistic "right to be left alone" is feasible. Rather, rights imply collective responsibility and obligations one to another. Some entities fulfill or fail these obligations without rational thought or consciousness, others do not, but the distinction is not particularly important.
6. All existence is a drive to be, and to change, which assumes and must be granted a basic legitimacy.

Art and the Natural Right of Expression

The philosopher Hans-Georg Gadamer argued that when a work of art is created, Being itself is increased. Similarly, sculptors frequently describe their work not as forcing material into some shape, but rather as releasing and re-alizing the potential form that was already present in the material. The sculptor assists the object in its development and self-expression. Arguing for the rights of nature leads to some exceptionally difficult problems that the enriching power of art might help us address.

If each thing has a right to exist due to its mere existence and path of de-velopment, a libertarian understanding of rights leads us into a rather striking form of nihilism. From this view, I can do nothing and change nothing without doing wrong. The ant I unknowingly tread upon today has been wronged. There is, however, something correct about elements of this view. All existence comes at a price to those things existing around us, and many aspects of the way most of us live today increase this price to unjust proportions. But the message of the rights of nature is not that all existence and action is wrong, but rather that all existence and action comes with responsibility. As parts of an interwoven cosmos seeking to joyfully express its nature, there is no exit from responsibility: we are, as Dostoyevsky puts it, "responsible for all to all."[103] How can I eat and end the life of the entity devoured? Only with a firm acceptance of my obligation to express more fully in my life the potential of that entity and a respect for its sacrifice.

In some art the material is devoured, destroyed in the making; but in the best art, in the truest art, the material comes more fully to life and expression. Art is the act of freeing the potential of what is, of augmenting and nurturing the growth and expression of existence, and it is this that nature demands of us. Neither master nor engineer nor illegitimate interloper, we are part of nature's living. We are called to take our part with loving devotion to the value of each and every other participant, be it tree, stone, bird, or star. This means an end to easy answers. If my interest is in having a nice clear list of forbidden and obligatory actions, I am going to be very disappointed. We should not be surprised at this, as responsibility comes hand in hand with the obligation to think carefully and risk failure.

---

103 Fydor Dostoyevsky, Pevear, and Volokhonsky, *The Brothers Karamazov* (New York City: Farrar, Straus, and Giroux, 2002), Part II, Book IV: Lacerations, Chapter 1: Father Ferapont: "For know, dear ones, that every one of us is undoubtedly responsible for all men -- and everything on earth... each one per-sonally for all mankind and every individual man."

At the most basic level, there is one natural right and it is shared by all things: the right to exist as a process of self-expression. It comes united with an obligation: the obligation to respect and assist the existence and self-expression of each thing around me. Sometimes this obligation will involve killing and destruction, but only in service to a greater expression of being. Most often it will involve nurturing and a loving service to the world and cosmos of which we are children.

Property

What does the right to existence and self-expression imply for other traditional rights? Most importantly, it implies that our concept of property and the right to property is deeply flawed.

Locke, and recent libertarian thinkers such as Robert Nozick, derive the right to property from the right to life (or existence, as I have been calling it). The idea is this: the right to life is a basic property right. I own my body and this body cannot be taken from me. This leads to the right to liberty, as my ownership over my body also means that my use of this body (with rather striking exceptions for Locke) cannot be limited. Now, when I work I use my body to transform something else. I invest some of my body (bodily energy and work) into the thing transformed. This makes the thing created part of my body in a limited sense. I have invested bodily life, so the thing becomes an extended part of my bodily life. When I grow apples, my use of my body in the work makes the apples part of me in a very limited sense, so my basic right to ownership over my body extends to the thing produced.[104]

The view I have presented contains a different conception of both work and the natural world, largely because of the rejection of anthropocentrism. When I grow a tree, it is as much the case that my body becomes part of the tree, part of its process of self-expression. The tree "owns" me just as much as I own it. But, even the concept of ownership is still incorrect here. From a perspective that does not prioritize reason (or the mind-soul over the body and natural existence), I can't be said to own my body. I *am* my body, it is not property. Similarly, without anthropocentrism and in light of pagan animism,

---

104 Interestingly, this is also the basis of much Marxist thought mediated through Hegel's adoption of similar conceptions of work through which the world becomes an expression of the self and, as it were, a second body. It is also worth noting that this is the basis of Locke's argument in favor of taking land from the Native Americans. They didn't work the land, he claimed, and so didn't gain ownership through transformation of it.

we cannot see the world as a collection of raw materials for use, nor can we imagine making a tree (or anything else) part of our bodies without thought to its own individual existence. The tree and I might be in partnership, but it does not become me and I do not become it. We are part of something larger, but neither dominates in the manner required for ownership. Furthermore, the tree is also in partnership with things other than myself, belying any claim to an exclusive relationship with it.

My right to self-expression also includes my right not to have my partnerships unduly interfered with and broken. You can't come along and chop down the tree I have worked to grow without weighty reasons, but it is wrong to think that this entity with an existence and nature of its own is "mine" in any robust sense, or that my relationship with it overpowers all other relationships it has. I have a right to have my relationships respected and protected, except when those relationships become unjustifiably abusive, dominating, or destructive. So, in an interconnected world viewed through the lens of the right to exist, the right to relationships replaces rights to property.

CHAPTER SEVEN
The Music of the Spheres:
Of Values, Paganism, and Capitalism

Wisdom does not reside in one head.
Traditional Akan Saying

As should now be clear, paganism is dedicated to the rich complexity, vibrancy, and value-laden nature of life. In our modern age, however, we have a highly subjective concept of value. We primarily understand value as what a thing has because it is valued by someone. From this reasoning, without human valuing nothing would have value. In other words, value has no reality in and of itself, but rather derives from human actions or resides in human minds alone. The model here, of course, is the little pieces of paper and metal that we make into valuable money because we treat them as such.

But the actual word for value, and the origins of the concept behind the word, comes from words for strength and power. Relative terms, surely, but not subjective ones. Value, valor, virtue, and virility all share the same origin in the Proto-Indo-European word walh or welh (meaning "strength") which became valere in Latin. Far from the model of money, their most primordial model is fire (another word which is cognate with value) and, we might suggest, the incontestable importance of light and the sun.

Value shines. It is that which shines-out to us, that which shines for us. It does not shine because we make it shine, but rather it calls to us as the sun draws the plant that leans towards it. Nature values because it responds to the obvious presence of real value. We might say that wherever there is the force of attraction there is value. The earth values the sun when the day-star sets its path and motivation.

Human values are no different: they are the draw of things of power and importance that appear to us and define us as those who can see them. Value, then, is inseparable from the concept of a calling. We do not, cannot, determine or choose what will call us. We can only listen, or refuse to listen, to the call.

Value and the Gods

If we contemplate the model of values as fire and as light, we see that values determine how the world shows up for us. Certain things leap out at us as important, worthy of respect, or in need of a response from us. Therefore, values are reality's opening of a conversation with us, a conversation to be enacted through what we do. The light determines the look of things, what shows up and what doesn't, how things appear. It is in the light of how reality reveals itself to me as value, worth, beauty, and truth that I become who I am and act upon the world as it has appeared.

One of the oldest forms of value are the goddesses and gods whose shining appearance casts the whole of reality into a certain aspect and form. Since before history, when values called to humanity they called through the voice of the divinities. When ancient heroes displayed valor or virtue, they were understood to embody or be empowered by one of the gods: they become the active body of value. In fact, this is what virtue first meant: to embody value; that is, the power and truth of a divinity. Far from subjective creations, value was understood to be the revealing of a truth most frequently encountered as a divinity.

This concrete and particular nature of value as a call coming to us from reality is a general characteristic of pagan ethics. While later ethical systems will attempt to reduce all actions in terms of various general and universal principles, pagan ethics is always contextual and particular. It is the call of the situation, the way that value shines within a moment of challenge, that determines whether or not we end up embodying divine value (virtue) in that situation. Sympathy and empathy, the call to stand-up and act, and the resistance to the glaring appearance of wrong are all at the heart of pagan ethics. The gods appear in particular ways, and they demand of us particular responses to the events we find ourselves in, in a way where no general rules or universal moral laws are possible. Virtue consists of seeing into the situation, catching the glimpse and glow of the meaning of the situation, and responding in turn to that shining truth.

This connection between values and divinities also explains the connection between divinities and nature. In the power and beauty of the river, the face of a goddess or god shines forth, the aspect of a value. The terror and force of the mountain or storm unveiled the might of some divinity and revealed a demand: a value. None of this is to suggest that divinities are *symbols* of values. We have emptied values of their active vitality and personality, and so find it hard to understand that values are experienced in the action and event of basic truths, forces, powers, and realities appearing to us. Values, as active agents, are better taken as symbols of the divinities, rather than the reverse.

The recognition of several diverse and separate divinities is the recognition that reality is made up of a plurality of irreducible forces and truths. There are always many values, and they cannot be translated one into another or reduced one to another. The many values, as the many gods, are incommensurable: they share no common measure against which they can be organized and unified. There is no unity, no totality, no final truth nor value.

Despite that, certain values and gods will call to each individual in a unique manner. I will serve certain divinities, enlightened by certain values, and you others. It is only together that we gain a better grasp of the endless plurality that is reality, but not through totalizing the diversity of values, truths and ways of life. The particularity of what calls to me versus what calls to you will be a marker of the different ongoing events of meaning, and indeed divine bodies, that we each find ourselves already part of or that we become part of through choice and action. To value is to be part of larger wholes, to be called by these larger wholes, which can be gods, communities, traditions, and meanings depending on which particular context we are speaking from.

Spheres of Being and Council

The plurality of divinities, each calling or manifesting for those with whom they share a particular connection, can perhaps best be captured in thinking about spheres of meaning and value. The sociologist Max Weber was a twentieth-century thinker who worked extensively on the idea of incommensurable spheres of meaning and value. He spoke in terms of the spheres of intellect, religion, economy, government, and aesthetics, amongst others. A member of any given sphere who dedicated their life and work to that sphere did so as a vocation.[105] Weber's concern, however, was that the extent to which these spheres are separate and incommensurable leads to ever increasing isolation of different types of power in specific hands. For example, he saw religious individuals increasingly withdrawing from participation in politics. He also saw an increasing impossibility of importing the ethics derived from other spheres of existence into the sphere of politics.

Similarly, he witnessed the increasing willingness of people to isolate their economic activity from the ethical standards they derived from other spheres. One could be cruel and cold in business and disregard the ethics one would normally follow in the rest of ones' life. "It's just business" or "it's just politics" becomes a catch phrase standing in for the increasing tendency to isolate what we value from what we do, along with insulating the values of one sphere from those of another. Weber, it is worth noting, was theorizing in the Weimer Republic in Germany while witnessing the rise of fascism.

By theorizing politics primarily in terms of bureaucratic positions and the general practice of "managing" society, Weber failed to appreciate some larger implications of his theories regarding multiplicities of spheres of politics. From a high pagan perspective, such as that captured in the Akan concept of wisdom through council, politics is the process of collectively benefiting from the plurality of value-spheres and negotiating the inevitable (and not inevitably negative) conflicts between spheres of value. If we are to take seriously the idea that "wisdom does not reside in one head," then we can only be wise to the extent that we collectively engage in council and benefit from the vocation of others. This is particularly important because, as mentioned, pagan metaphysics assumes the inevitability of conflict. The goal is to keep the conflict amongst different ways of life, divine dictates, values, and so on as productive as possible.

Consider, once more, the example of the conflict that arises in *The Oresteia*. Here we have murder, vengeance killings, and very real conflicts amongst different values, concepts of justice, and divinities. On both the local and cosmic levels, the conflict here could not be more dangerous and delicate. Recall that the gods in conflict, the Furies and Apollo, represent the two major orders of divine governance and this conflict could easily reignite full-scale war amongst the gods. The questions of how the vengeance killings could ever end and whether the cities of Greece are to know peace amongst the

---

105 See Weber's "Politics as Vocation," "Science as Vocation," and "Religious Rejections of the World and Their Directions" for key examples of this type of thinking in Weber.

followers of different divinities are at stake as well.

Apollo turns to Athena to solve the situation but her first answer is a failed one. Her answer is to invent a majoritarian jury system to decide the case. The problem is that, once the ruling goes against the Furies, they decide to turn against the earth itself and curse all of humanity. In other words, a system with winners and losers such as a majoritarian democracy can't avoid the most extreme forms of conflict. A sufficiently polarized situation will lead inevitably to slaughter and chaos even, or especially, with a majoritarian system. This precise argument has been used against majoritarian democracies in Africa by both Wiredu and Kwami Gyekye. When you have territories artificially formed into singular nation states but containing different communities with different ways of life, a majoritarian democracy is exceptionally dangerous, because the minority communities will either always be dominated by the majority or will be left with no choice but violent resistance.[106]

Athena's eventual solution to this situation is to move towards consensus and real council instead. She cannot overturn the jury's judgment, nor would she wish to, but she can provide the Furies with an important place within the justice system and governing of Athens. It is ultimately an insufficient answer, but it works for the specific situation. A fuller move towards consensus and council would be necessary for a lasting solution. Of course, a system of consensus councils like in the Akan society is not a perfect solution to political issues. Consensus requires a culture of discussion and debate that aims sincerely at agreement.

In other words, without a pagan metaphysics that recognizes the fundamental value of different views and, in fact, the unavoidableness of these differences and the incompleteness of one's own position, consensus would be impossible. A winner-takes-all culture, a culture in which it is possible to believe one is entirely right, is already one that is broken. One must come to council assuming, from the start, that one has something to learn.

This is why Liberal Democracy is an insufficient answer. The metaphysical basis of Liberal Democracy is the idea that rational self-determination is the highest value and is best preserved by allowing for collective decision-making and protected spheres of personal choice. The overall assumption, though, is that there is one right answer to any question. In Liberal Democracy, debate

---

106 See Chapter 14 "Democracy and Consensus: A Plea for a Non-Party Polity" in Wiredu's *Cultural Universals and Particulars* and Chapter 2 "Person and Community: In Defense of Moderate Communitarianism," Chapter 3 "Ethnicity, Identity, and Nationhood," and Chapter 4 "Traditional Political Ideas, Values, and Practices: Their Status in the Modern Setting" in Gyekye's *Tradition and Modernity*.

and discussion are not good in themselves but rather exist for the sake of allowing for the space in which people will have the chance to arrive at the right answer. You can witness similar perspectives with people committed to absolutist religious views who, nonetheless, do not wish to use power to force their views on others. They are certain they are right, and have nothing to learn from others, but want to kindly grant you the free space in which to discover that they are right. Pagan metaphysics, on the other hand, points to there being no one position that is or can be complete, total, and "right." The "right" answer does not reside in any one head or sphere of meaning, whether mine or yours.

A robust system of consensus requires particular personal involvement in the process, and so would require a redistribution of political power to very small local levels. While councils can be made up of representatives chosen by the people, these representatives must be actually and practically answerable to the people who, in turn, are able to be aware of and review the reasoning and decisions made by the representatives. In other words, representative systems only work to respect difference when they are based on very small-scale communities and avoid the need for majoritarian systems in selecting the representative and judging their decisions.[107]

Dominance and Monopoly

This basic commitment to the value of other ways of life, to the wisdom contained amongst the full diversity of values and truths, is perhaps the fundamental treasure a pagan metaphysics offers us. It is very far from our monotheistic culture, in which we all assume, to a greater or lesser degree, that we have a monopoly on being right. Unfortunately, our problems run deeper than just questions of how to organize our government. We face deep cultural resistance, which is to say metaphysical resistance, to the existence of a true society of pluralism. This is unavoidably connected to what are arguably the two most powerful manifestations of a monotheistic metaphysics: totalitarianism and Capitalism.

In order to more fully appreciate this claim it is necessary to go beyond We-

---

107 Perhaps, ideally, no representation would be used if we could base decision-making on local enough councils. These are, of course, just reflections and ruminations upon what a politics modeled on council might look like. There will undoubtedly be a plurality of such systems and how they arise and are to be structured will depend on the environment in which they form and the people and values they involve.

ber's conception of spheres of value. The contemporary political philosopher, Michael Walzer, has built a rather interesting theory of justice that is useful for our purposes. This system is presented in Walzer's book *Spheres of Justice: A Defense of Pluralism and Equality*. This book is dedicated to considerations of distributive justice, the question of how various goods should be distributed in a society in order for that society to be just. Amongst these goods, we could list such things as: wealth, political power, religious rank, intellectual influence, medical treatment, housing, food, education, love, travel, and so on.

Walzer's surprisingly simple proposal is that different goods each have their own logic of distribution; that is, they each have their own way of being distributed such that the distribution would be just. A society can be evaluated in terms of how goods are distributed within their own sphere and in terms of how these spheres relate to each other. Walzer points out that most political and economic theory, as well as law, has focused on the question of monopoly within given spheres, while largely ignoring the relationship between spheres. It is when a person, or group of people, monopolize a given sphere that there is likely to be resistance and a push for redistribution. Walzer suggests that the real problem, however, comes from the dominance of one sphere over the others rather than monopolies within spheres. Here is the general breakdown Walzer gives of three possible positions on the question of distribution:

1. The claim that the dominant good, whatever it is, should be redistributed so that it can be equally or at least more widely shared: this amounts to saying that monopoly is unjust.
2. The claim that the way should be opened for the autonomous distribution of all social goods: this amounts to saying that dominance is unjust.
3. The claim that some new good, monopolized by some new group, should replace the currently dominant good: this amounts to saying that the existing pattern of dominance and monopoly is unjust.[108]

Most developed nations, and especially the United States, are ones in which control of capital is the dominant good. In other words, access to political power, religious rank, intellectual influence, medical care, education, and so on, are largely determined by access to or relation to the sphere of wealth. This, in other words, captures the nature of Capitalism. All goods are market goods, understood in terms of one ultimate value: that of wealth or control over capital.

---

108 Michael Walzer, *Spheres of Justice: A Defense of Pluralism and Equality* (New York: Basic Books, 2010), 13.

Walzer suggests that people fighting against the dominance of capital in our society largely make the mistake of relying upon the first or third claim. The first amounts to saying that it is just fine that education and health are distributed based on monetary concerns, but wealth should be more fairly distributed rather than being monopolized by the current highly entrenched upper classes. Walzer identifies the third claim with the common forms of Communism and Marxism, such that the dominance of one given sphere is fine but this sphere should not be that of ownership over capital and the means or production.

Walzer prefers the second claim, namely that monopoly within spheres can be justifiable but it is the dominance of the spheres by some one sphere (which comes to be considered the dominant good) that really causes the problem. The problem isn't that capital tends to be isolated in the hands of the few. It is instead that this also means that power in all the other spheres is also isolated in those hands. If money had nothing to do with political influence, or access to healthcare, housing, and food, or intellectual influence, or access to education, etc., it wouldn't be a problem at all if the few held most of the capital. Indeed, in a society that fully and consistently fought for the autonomy of different spheres of goods, the hoarding of capital could be seen as little more than a rather odd obsession in the same way we might consider fantasy football to be a rather mystifying past time.

Walzer's perspective does not perfectly capture my own, but it does provide us with a way to discuss different spheres of value. From a pagan perspective, society suffers from injustice when the (likely unconscious) followers of Hermes in the sphere of trade determine whether, and how, one can serve Apollo through the pursuit of poetry. Similarly, the absolute dominance of the sphere of Zeus (i.e., political power) over Hermes' sphere of trade would amount to an injustice as well as would, as in our society, the dominance of material wealth and trade over political power.[109] Our current situation is one in which spheres of value are almost entirely dominated by one sphere alone.

Such a dominance of one sphere over others is inevitable for a society caught in a monotheistic metaphysics. If the universe is ultimately ruled by the One—and the path of purity, obedience, and virtue is the narrow path towards this One—there will inevitably be a basic value that organizes all the others. The forces of reduction and totalization demand society bows to the rule of some One sphere as capturing the nature of the divine.

---

109 I am, of course, dramatically simplifying the correspondence of various spheres of value to gods. I recognize the distinctions here are far more fine-grained.

Capitalism, Monotheism, and Nihilism

Capitalism is necessarily monotheist in its metaphysics: it reduces all values to one ultimate value, specifically the standard of price. The market admits the fact that people will value different things and will disagree about a given thing's value, but one element is asserted (and echoed in economics) without question: all things will be reducible to a price people are willing to pay. We see obvious examples of this in terms of risk calculations that determine how many people can be injured or killed by a product before the cost gets too expensive for a company. Human lives, pain, suffering, and death can all be reduced to a price. So too can environmental destruction. How much profit, it is asked, can be extracted from the earth before the destruction outweighs the benefit? Forest and mountains, entire species and nations, all have their price. For the market and the Capitalist there is absolutely nothing which cannot be numbered, calculated: that is, price checked. In this sense Capitalism is leveling, it levels the diversity of values to the basic point of price.

We should avoid assuming that Capitalism places wealth or profit as the ultimate value to which all others may be reduced. For many, the goal might be wealth or profit, but the illusory nature of wealth is inherent to Capitalism's own system. Money is just worthless paper and metal unless people behave as if it is not, and the wealthiest people and wealthiest businesses have far more money than the search for wealth would really justify.

Wealth is a finite value, but Capitalist leveling knows no end. Wealth is finite in the sense that it can only be used and enjoyed up to a certain point; beyond that point you have more than you can use, or you have too much for there to be anything (or anyone) left to buy. A society made up of three wildly wealthy people and a hoard of the desperately poor is a society in poverty for poor and rich alike: there will be nothing to own because nothing is produced and there will be no one to sell it to. This is why the collapse of the middle class is always the death knell for those who value wealth.

Capitalism knows no limit because it isn't about wealth, it is about power and control. The rise of Capitalism wasn't about the desire and the valuing of wealth conquering all other values; it was about certain social classes and members of professions attempting to gain power over other classes and roles. In this sense, the dream of Capitalism and science are similar: complete and total control, the ability to order and measure all things. This move from profit to control is the move from leveling to nihilism. We might, similarly, understand it as a transition from trade to The Market.

To understand this transition, it will be necessary to briefly turn our eyes to Karl Marx and the analysis he offers in *Capital*. Money and trade have been around for a long time, long before Capitalism. The most ancient cultures engaged in trade and had gods of trade. But despite the existence of money, trade wasn't about profit measured in cash, it was about concrete diverse goods. In *Capital*, Marx lays out two primary and different processes in which money might function. First, and most ancient, is the use of money as a medium for exchange. We can represent this in the following way in terms of Money (M) and the concrete goods of Commodities (C):

C -> M -> C

This process represents the use of a good you have (for instance, grain you have grown), to arrive at money through trade that is then used to purchase another good such as shoes.

This is the same basic process as direct trade of goods, where grain would be exchanged for shoes, but money as a medium allows for a wider range of trade: it can be used to buy many things, and so doesn't require the grain producer to find a shoe maker in need of grain. The goal here is goods, or commodities, and the process can be used in service of any set of values, since various values can be served through the goods/commodities we aim to purchase. This process can also be in service to wealth, as the collective commodities the process aims at might be those of luxury, riches and so on. This is what most people think goes on it the market, which misses the fundamental nature of Capitalism.

The above ancient process transforms in more modern Capitalism into this process:

M -> C -> M

Here, the goal of the process and the starting position of the process are different. We begin with money, and use it to purchase commodities (or the means to produce commodities) in order to then sell the commodity for a profit. It is only here that profit can make sense and is the idea of investment, the process through which one uses money to make money. While in the first process the diversity of values determines what might be worth pursuing for yourself, the second process equates all goods and values to a basic monetary value.

These two processes can be distinguished in terms of use-value versus exchange-value. A thing's use-value is how much it is worth to any given person based on their needs and desires: "how valuable are shoes to me at this time?" It is not a type of value that is easily or naturally reduced to a number. A thing's exchange-value, on the other hand, is the amount of money I can get for it when selling it. It makes sense to say that, at this time, shoes have the same use-value for me as a pair of pants but not as much value as a new computer. But we cannot say this of exchange-value, which is always immediately presented in terms of money and can only be tied to goods through a secondary process.

We can see the contrast between these two processes clearly if we consider the difference between ancient trade (and the values it frequently served) and the modern Market economy. Ancient trade was most distinctly in service of diversity and plurality. Its gods, such as Janus and Hermes, were gods of new beginnings and doorways. Trade was united unavoidably with travel, so the gods of trade were also the gods of travel. The collection of values which group around these related ideas of newness, beginnings, openness, and travel make clear that trade was undertaken in the spirit of curiosity and cultural enrichment rather than strictly of profit or wealth. The image of ancient trade was the wild diversity of the agora marketplace or bazaar. The marketplace was a failure if it lacked a pluralism of goods and life. Money, while perhaps used for exchange (though not always so used), hardly features into it at all.

In contrast, the image of the modern Market is the bank or stock exchange replete with numbers and abstract symbols of exchange-value: money. An ancient marketplace can't function without diversity and strangeness, but the modern Market does not require diversity. This is why it is possible to use money to buy money and then, in turn, to make money from the exchange. This is what happens in currency exchanges, or the purchasing and selling of debt. The modern Market can be strictly empty of commodities and still function, because what is being bought and sold are certain patterns of money.

It is not just that the modern Market doesn't require diversity of goods. Rather, it actively militarizes against it. Since all things on the Market must be reduced to price, (that is, exchange-value), there is already inherent in the Market a basic drive towards interchangeability and similarity. Things that are too new or too odd become difficult to price, so must be either dismissed from the Market or made to conform to the Market's prices. In contemporary Capitalism the world is the Market, and vice versa, so all things must be reduced and ordered. Even "priceless" works of art are insured for specific amounts.

The fact that money can be exchanged and priced makes clear that the final goal of Capitalism and its world market is not money, wealth, or profit. The goal is order, and order of a very special sort. The Market's goal is an ordered world in which all things are reduced to their Market price, a world in which one need never deal with faces, textures, sights, or feelings but rather numbers alone. The essence of the Capitalist Market is the force of translation and reduction, the ultimate force of monotheistic abstraction, the apotheosis of writing's influence upon human thought.

In this it shares an essence with modern industrial science, whose goal is the reduction of all things to raw materials from which power (much like price) is to be extracted and transformed. Mountain to coal, coal to energy, energy to work and so on, the process of transformation pursues only its own growth so that anything that is produced is produced only to increase the power of production. Ultimately, abstract power seeks only its own growth without end or purpose, and this growth of power is a process of leveling or pricing.

It is precisely this lack of goal or purpose that represents the nihilistic nature of the Capitalist Market. It knows no goal and no specific values. It is entirely abstract. It is without commitment. In this sense, it is also without actors. The C.E.O. is a tool of the ongoing growth and ordering of the Market as much as anyone else is. There is no place outside the process, and so no ultimate leader or beneficiary of it. Even the richest and most powerful people in the world have a very specific market value that marks the point at which they can be annihilated or exchanged for someone or something else.

The Market process is a process without limit. It will allow and can calculate the price and profit of any action. Cities and nations have a price, as indeed the Capitalist resistance to acting on climate change makes clear, as do the Capitalist machinations leading to warfare. The day will come when the full planet will have a price, once the possibility of moving elsewhere becomes a reality. We will soon know at what price Gaia can be bought and sold.

Capitalism versus Character

A true commitment to a given value or set of values marks the limit of action beyond which a person will not go. These ultimate defining commitments constitute any given person's character. Discover what is most important to a person, what they will never harm or destroy, what they will die for the sake of, and you have uncovered that person's character. The Market has no such limit, and those that will always do what the Market reveals as profitable likewise have no character. They exist in a world in which the call of reality—its revelation in terms of beauty, divinity, or truth—is ignored as impractical.

In this way, we can see that the Market requires a dramatic ignorance of reality and truth which results in divorcing what it insists is "practical," "profitable," and "reasonable" from what is grounded in reality and the world. The Market is a phantom, an illusory claw, a mathematical dream of abstraction run hopelessly awry. It demands that we ignore everything that calls to us as worth pursuing or preserving, all that we are drawn to love and revere. For many of us this is the earth and its children: animal, plant, and human. Also, it might be the full richness of different ways of life, various cultures, complex history, the spectrum of visions revealing the wild complexity of meanings and values. It might, as well, be something as simple as human sympathy and empathy, that most impractical value of all. In the face of the Market the pagan says "no" to the dominance of any one value and "no" to a limitless nihilistic process of destruction and control. Here is our character where we draw the line and state clearly that some things, many things, even most things, have no market price. We live in the priceless world because it is a world of real values not open to exchange.

The nihilism of Capitalism comes about through a rather surprising historical process grounded firmly in monotheism. If Capitalism replaces the idea that "wisdom does not reside in one head" with the claim that "wisdom resides in the market" it is because of the hidden religious and metaphysical basis of Capitalism's seductive force. In *The Protestant Ethic and the Spirit of Capitalism*, Weber shows that Capitalism takes its primary importance in the modern world through its derivation from the Protestant obsession with finding worldly signs of having been saved. Because it was largely believed that whom god would redeem couldn't be determined through one's actions or character, it was taken as a sign of god's favor to be prosperous and rich. This, in turn, meant that wealth was not desired for its own sake but instead was desired as a mark of salvation.

To return to our earlier considerations of purity, obedience, and the one narrow path to holiness, Capitalism derives is strength from market success becoming a sign of spiritual purity. As the actual outward religious aspects of monotheism faded in society, the underlying sense that market success marked one out as particularly good, pure, and in line with the One Truth remained nonetheless. This accounts, largely, for the strangely obsessive and pathological nature that monetary success takes on in late Capitalist societies. One hoards more than one could ever need or want, one fails to really enjoy what one gains, yet one continues to gluttonously gain and hoard, gain and hoard. There remains, in the mind of the good Capitalist—especially at their very highest ranks—the perverse conviction that in gathering their absurd amounts of wealth and power they are somehow proving their inherent value and saving their souls.

Even though there is not a thing that they or the Market ultimately value beyond the blind and dumb process of accumulation itself, still they long to be part of some real meaningful value. It is this same aspect that accounts for Capitalism's own inability to show any real concern for the growing inevitability of worldwide devastation due to climate change. While the religious Right might piously state that, if climate change is real, then god will take care of it, the Capitalist piously assumes something similar. In the perception of the super wealthy, consumption and accumulation will eventually solve this problem as well. We witness, as it were, cancer hoping that further growth will keep the cancer from killing its host.

There is a sense in which monotheism was always nihilistic. It always identified the ultimate value as one that was so abstract and transcendental as to be without content. It should not be surprising that its ultimate contemporary manifestation should be one that is both without respect for any value whatsoever and also so deeply destructive. When ultimate value is located beyond the boundaries of anything we live or can know, remaining committed to such a value becomes cruelty and spite towards the world of lesser values. It is this perspective that allows one to torture and kill for the sake of "saving the souls" of those who are tortured and killed. It is the perspective that allows slavery and genocide to be understood as blessings which went hand in hand with the transcendental salvation of the enslaved and murdered.

Transcendence is a funhouse mirror, in which everything good in this world becomes bad in the eyes of the transcendent and everything good in the name of transcendence implies a horror here in this world. Suffering as salvation. Murder as kindness. Starvation and slavery as purification. Obedience as freedom. And, ultimately, freedom as sin and damnation.

CONCLUSION

The dangerous forces that threaten life and joy here on earth are intimately connected with the changes that began with the rise of writing and loss of high pagan metaphysics. The world of living value, the web of ultimately important relationships that define us, an embodied world of vibrant active meaning, is the world we can reclaim.

Investigating high pagan cultures is a necessary step to reclaiming this world. Our internalized monotheistic metaphysics and its abstract illusions blind us from seeing the life around us. The world of lifeless matter and alienated consciousness, a dead world of raw materials reducible to price, is one swiftly drawing to its own destruction.

A pagan worldview is one open to the concrete immediacy of the cosmos that surrounds it. It does not reduce reality to lifeless abstractions such as energy, or order, or matter, or resource, or price, or property, perfection, or singular Truth. A living animist world of actions and events, rather than matter or consciousness, is one in which understanding ourselves and the rich meaning possible for our lives requires that we understand our relationships to the world around us.

Blessedly impure, richly interconnected, irreducibly pluralistic, this world and cosmos calls to each of us to act, but it calls in many voices and for many actions. Only when we can be many—and when our love and commitment is tied to the multitude that is reality—can we be free in complex communities of difference. Only then can the world be something other than a source of meaningless raw material and a torture chamber for meaningless lives defined only by the drive to own because we have lost the chance to live.

Ultimately the rich insights we need are farthest from the traditional centers of imperial power and closest to those whom empire has most cruelly destroyed and dominated. Far from the illusory impossible center, it is those with the least voice who most need to be heard.

I have not given concrete recipes for a reinvention of politics; only collectively can we find the wisdom necessary for such an endeavor. A pagan metaphysics calls for a rethinking of the concept of rights and for the autonomy of spheres of value. This means those committed to these spheres of meaning need to take a stand at the place where they cannot be bought and will not be bullied into backing down. Each person who would find themselves committed to a god, to a purpose, to a meaning in the pluralistic abundance of a pagan cosmos must ask themselves where such a place is, a place where they can state "here I stand and will not be moved." What is your limit and the commitment that forms your character? From there we can enter into communal council about what is to be done.

The metaphysics embodied in the societies in which we currently live cannot provide the basis for meaningful lives open to real living values. Instead, it substitutes lack of meaning and pathological obsessions with abstract wealth and property. To be in touch with the divinity of a living cosmos has been replaced in our society with the dream of being rich. The rich, too many believe, are the saved, the good, the beautiful, the true. One's bank account and investment portfolio is the ledger of the soul, or what remains of the soul. The enslavement of every part of our lives to economy, and the demand that one must work to live (even though most of our jobs are unnecessary and empty) is both dehumanizing and a brutal distortion of reality. It is also unsustainable. As argued in Chapter Six, our very concept of ownership and the right to property disfigures our relationship to the world and brutalizes the living reality around us.

The utter dominance of economy mirrors other distinctly modern authoritarian attempts to order society according to one ultimate truth, just as monotheistic religions have attempted to order all of society in terms of their own conceptions of ultimate truth. The mistaken assumption that science provides privileged access to the nature of reality, and the power this view grants industry and technology to organize and tyrannize society, is one such reductive process.[110] Similarly, the idea that the value sphere of politics, or of eco-

---

110 Science does not have to be totalizing, there are thinkers such as Karen Barad, Thomas Kuhn, Paul Feyerabend and Ernst Mach who recognized its own potential for a multitude of epistemic approaches

nomics, should dominate over the distribution of all other goods levels the world and deadens our lives.

Each of us house within ourselves a similar tyrant born of monotheistic metaphysics, a voice that tells as that, though we might be perfectly willing to allow others to believe and live as they wish, they are ultimately wrong and we know the one final truth. Openness to the voices of the cosmos, to the wisdom of others who see what we do not and know what we cannot, to the living earth desperately calling out to us, is more than anything how we must learn once more to live.

The internalized monotheistic worldview in every aspect of our societies atomizes us. We become consciousness cut off from other consciousnesses. We are cut off also from our own bodies, bodies of lifeless chemicals cut off from a world of meaning. We become isolated and alienated. Paganism can teach that we are not ultimately minds, even if those minds are understood in terms of souls, just as we are not ultimately brute collections of matter. We are interconnected events of meaning, expressions of a living earth and living cosmos. The abstractions that currently structure our lives, whether the economic calculations that find their apotheosis in The Market or political voting percentages, are mere attempts to order meaningless atoms which interact in the void of what our societies have become.

But we are not atoms and there is no void. Majoritarian democracy is a manifestation of this distorted view of reality, a way to reduce a multitude to one, to create winners and losers out of a plurality. There are and have been other methods truer to the cosmos' rich diversity: the Akan model of council is one such model, as are consensus approaches to democracy.

We have uncovered some of the rich understanding of a living cosmos that can allow us to resist the objectifying and alienating forces of leveling and domination. We can rediscover what it is to live with, in, and through the earth in the company of the gods and in continuity with all the living and the dead. The promise of oral thought rather than abstraction, pagan animism rather than reductive materialism or consciousness focused idealism, and the ever-growing abundance of a relational event ontology all serve to open the road towards new ways of life. If we are to survive, if beautiful burgeoning diversity is to survive, much of what has been lost to us must be regained. We must learn, once more, to listen to this world around us.

---

and fundamental assumptions. This is not, however, the path that science's role in our contemporary world has taken.

This, then, is my wish and hope for you, my reader. May you look upon a living cosmos of unpredictable and unstoppable change. May you hear, in this wild and free event of naturing, the songs and call of the gods. May your bodies dance with theirs, embraced by values that light your world and life with the inspiration of communion with living embodied divinities. And this, above all else, I beseech you: *remain true to the earth*. Then, collectively, may we go forth to fight for her and for each other. This, above all: remain true to the earth.

BIBLIOGRAPHY

A.A. Barb "Three Elusive Amulets" JWCI 27 (1964).

Aeschylus, and A. J. Bowen. *Aeschylus: Suppliant Women*. Liverpool: Liverpool University Press, 2013.

Aeschylus, and Hugh Lloyd-Jones. *The Eumenides by Aeschylus*. Englewood Cliffs, NJ: Prentice-Hall, 1970.

Augustine, *The City of God Against the Pagans*. Cambridge: Cambridge University Press, 1998.

Barad, Karen Michelle. *Meeting the Universe Halfway: Quantum Physics and the Entanglement of Matter and Meaning*. Durham: Duke University Press, 2007.

Betz, Hans Dieter. *The Greek Magical Papyri*. Chicago: Chicago Univ. Press, 1986.

Bray, Olive, and W. G. Collingwood. *The Poetic Edda: Illustrated - Original Text with English Translation - including a Glossary of Terms*. Brighton, Vic.: Leaves of Gold Press, 2013.

Bromwich, Rachel. Trioedd Ynys Prydein. Cardiff: Univ. of Wales Press.

Cicero. *De Natura Deorum* II.72.

Cohen, Carl, and Tom Regan. *The Animal Rights Debate*. Lanham: Rowman & Littlefield Publishing, 2001.

Crowley, Aleister. *Osmi Aetir I Liber Samekh*.

Dostoyevsky, Fydor, Pevear, and Volokhonsky. The Brothers Karamazov. New York City: Farrar, Straus, and Giroux, 2002.

DuBois, Page. *A Million and One Gods: The Persistence of Polytheism*. Cambridge, MA: Harvard University Press, 2014.

Graeber, David. *Debt: The First 5000 Years.* Haryana, India: Penguin Books, 2014.

Gyekye, Kwame. *An Essay on African Philosophical Thought: The Akan Conceptual Scheme.* Philadelphia: Temple University Press, 1995.

Gyekye, Kwame. *Tradition and Modernity: Philosophical Reflections on the African Experience.* New York: Oxford University Press, 2011.

Havelock, Eric Alfred. *Preface to Plato.* Cambridge, MA: Belknap Press, 1998.

Havelock, Eric Alfred. *The Muse Learns to Write: Reflections on Orality and Literacy from Antiquity to the Present.* New Haven: Yale University Press, 2005.

Havelock, Eric Alfred. *The Muse Learns to Write.* Yale University Press, 1986.

Heraclitus, and T.M. Robinson. Fragments. Toronto: Univ. of Toronto Press, 1987.

Hesiod, and Hugh G. Evelyn-White. *Homeric Hymns. Epic Cycle. Homerica.* Cambridge, MA: Harvard University Press, 1936.

Hesiod, and Lambardo, Stanley. Works and Days and Theogony. Indianapolis: Hackett Publishing Company, 1993.

Hesiod, Stephanie A. Nelson, Richard S. Caldwell. *Theogony ; And, Works and Days.* Newburyport, MA: Focus Publishing, 2009.

Hobbes, Thomas. *De Cive.*

Homer, and Lattimore. Iliad. Chicago: Univ. of Chicago Press, 2011.

Homer, Robert Fitzgerald, and Seamus Heaney. *The Odyssey.* London: David Campbell Publishers, 2000.

Huggens, Kim. "The Truth about Zombies, or: How to Survive the Zombie Apocalypse," *Memento Mori: A Collection of Magickal and Mythological Perspectives on Death, Dying, Mortality and Beyond.* London: Avalonia, 2012.

Johnston, Sarah Iles. *Hekate Soteira: A Study of Hekates Roles in the Chaldean Oracles and Related Literature.* Atlanta: Scholars Press, 1990.

Kadmus. "Nature's Rights," *A Beautiful Resistance: Everything We Already Are. Gods and Radicals,* 2015.

Kadmus. "Neo-Chthonia," *Fenris Wolf,* issue 8. Trapart, 2016.

King, Richard. *Orientalism and Religion: Postcolonial Theory, India and the "Mystic East."* London: Routledge, 2009.

Lactantius. *Institutiones Divinae* IV.28.

Law of Mother Nature Article 5, Bolivian Law.

Lesher, J. H., "Xenophanes of Colophon, Fragments: A Text and Translation with a Commentary," Toronto: Univ. of Toronto Press.

Lucan, and Jane Wilson Joyce. Pharsalia. Ithaca: Cornell Univ. Press, 1993.

Matthews, John. *Taliesin: The Last Celtic Shaman*. Rochester, VT: Inner Traditions, 2002.

Nussbaum, Martha Craven. *Creating Capabilities: The Human Development Approach*. Cambridge, MA: Belknap Press of Harvard University Press, 2011.

Plato and Reeve, Cratylus. Indianapolis: Hackett Publishing Company, 1998.

Plato, Benjamin Jowett, and Albert A. Anderson. *Platos Ion and Meno: Benjamin Jowetts Translation*. Millis, MA: Agora Publications, 1998.

Plato, G. M. A. Grube, and John M. Cooper. *The Trial and Death of Socrates: Euthyphro, Apology, Crito, Death Scene from Phaedo*. Indianapolis, IN: Hackett Pub., 1975.

Regan, Tom. Animal Rights, Human Wrongs: An Introduction to Moral Philosophy. Lanham, MD: Rowman & Littlefield, 2003.

Robinson, T. M. Heraclitus. University of Toronto Press, 1987.

Shelmerdine, Susan Chadwick. "Homeric Hymn to Apollo," The Homeric Hymns. Brantford, Ont.: W. Ross MacDonald School Resource Services Library, 2008.

Shelmerdine, Susan Chadwick. "Homeric Hymn to Hermes," The Homeric Hymns. Brantford, Ont.: W. Ross MacDonald School Resource Services Library, 2008.

Singer, Peter. Animal Liberation. New York: Harper Perennial modern Classics. 2009.

Singer, Peter. Practical Ethics. Cambridge: Cambridge University Press, 2017.

Spinoza, Benedictus De, and Michael L. Morgan. The Essential Spinoza: Ethics and Related Writings. Indianapolis: Hackett Pub., 2006.

Stratton-Kent, Jake. Geosophia: The Argo of Magic: From the Greeks to the Grimoires. Dover: Scarlet Imprint/Bibliothèque Rouge, 2010.

Stratton-Kent, Jake. The Headless One. United States: Hadean Press, 2012.

The Red book of Hergest

The White book of Rhydderch

Thompson, Christopher Scott. Pagan Anarchism. Gods and Radicals, 2016.

Tully, Caroline. "Demeter's Wrath: How the Eleusinian Mysteries Attempted to Cheat Death," Memento Mori: A Collection of Magickal and Mythological Perspectives on Death, Dying, Mortality and Beyond. London: Avalonia, 2012.

Virgil, Robert Fitzgerald, and Philip R. Hardie. The Aeneid. London: David Campbell Publishers, 2000.

Walzer, Michael. Spheres of Justice: A Defense of Pluralism and Equality. New York: Basic Books, 2010.

Weber, Gerth, and Mills. From Max Weber: Essays in Sociology. Oxford: Oxford Univ. Press, 1958.

White, Gordon. The Chaos Protocols: Magical Techniques for Navigating the New Economic Reality. Woodbury: Llewellyn Publications, 2016.

Wiredu, Kwasi. Cultural Universals and Particulars: An African Perspective. Bloomington: Indiana University Press, 1996.

Wiredu, Kwasi. Cultural Universals and Particulars: An African Perspective. Bloomington: Indiana University Press, 1996.

INDEX

B

C

D

E

F

G

L

M

N

O

P

W

X

Y

Z

ABOUT THE AUTHOR

Kadmus is a practicing ceremonial magician with a long-standing relationship to several pagan divinities, especially the ancient Celtic deities. His interests and practice are highly eclectic, but a deep commitment to paganism is the bedrock upon which they all rest. Kadmus is also an academic with a Ph.D. in philosophy. He has presented papers and published on the philosophical importance of the oral origins of the Homeric epics, amongst several other topics, and teaches at the college level.